UNDERSTANDING
C A T S

UNDERSTANDING
CATS

Their History, Nature and Behavior

ROGER TABOR

THE READER'S DIGEST ASSOCIATION, INC.
Pleasantville, New York/Montreal

In memory of my old cat Mr. Jeremy Fisher, who was almost 25 years old when she died; in celebration of Leroy and Tabitha, my present moggies; to record my congratulations to my parents on their 50 years of marriage; and to thank them for bringing me up in a household with cats and dogs, so that I could gain some understanding of both.

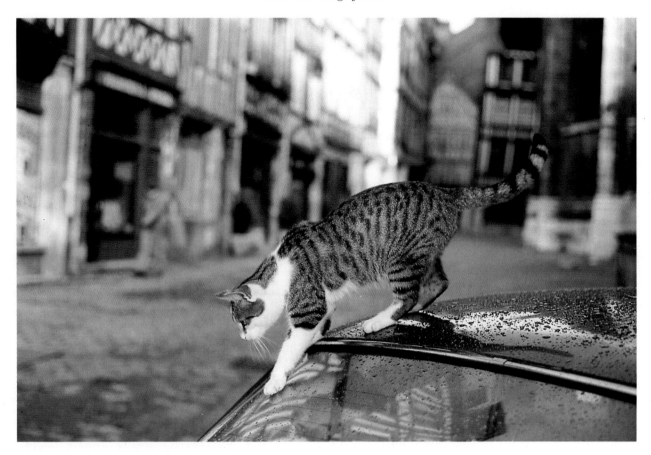

VIDEOS: BBC TV: *Cats* series and *Understanding Cats* series; Cats on Film/Avalon Productions: *Understanding Your Cat; Breaking Bad Habits for Cats; The Cat Outdoors; The Cat Indoors; Complete Cat Care; The Mystery of the Cat.*

AUDIO TAPES: "Focus on Ferals" seminar audio pack (Alley Cat Allies, USA, 1994).

PICTURE CREDITS
Roger Tabor 1, 2, 7 top right and top left, 8 right, 9, 11, 12, 13, 14, 15, 16,18, 19, 20, 21, 22, 23, 24 bot., 25, 26, 27, 28, 31, 32, 33, 36, 37, 38, 39, 40, 41, 42, 43, 44, 45, 48, 49, 50, 53, 54, 55, 56 top, 58 top, 59, 60, 61, 64, 66 bot., 68, 69, 70, 71, 72, 73, 74, 75, 76, 77, 78, 79, 84, 85, 87, 88, 89, 90, 91, 92, 93, 94, 95, 96, 97, 98, 99, 100, 101, 102, 104, 106, 111, 112, 113, 114, 115, 116, 117 top, 118 top, 121 top, 122, 126, 127, 129, 130, 132, 133, 134, 136, 139, 141; **Liz Artindale** 5, 7 bot. left and bot. right, 8 left, 10, 17, 24 top, 30, 34, 46, 47, 51, 52, 56 bot., 57, 58, 62, 63, 65, 66 top, 80, 81, 82, 83, 107, 109, 110, 117 bot., 118 left, 119, 120, 121 bot., 124, 125, 128, 131, 135, 137, 138, 140; **Judy Zukoski** 105

A READER'S DIGEST BOOK
Edited and produced by David & Charles Publishers

Book design by Chris Leishman Design
Text Copyright © Roger Tabor 1995

First published in Great Britain 1995
U.S. edition published 1997

Library of Congress Cataloging in Publication Data

Tabor, Roger K.
    Understanding cats : their history, nature and behavior / Roger Tabor.
        p.   cm.
    "A Reader's digest book"—T.p. verso.
    Includes bibliographical references (p.142) and index.
    ISBN 0-89577-916-1
    1. Cats. 2. Cats—History. 3. Cats—Behavior. I. Title.
SF442.T33 1997
636.8—dc20   96-25121
                                                          CIP

Contents

Foreword

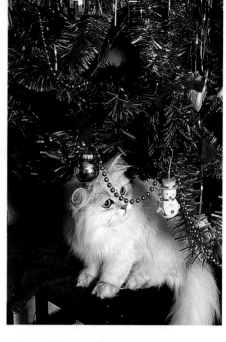

The key to understanding cats is to look at the many aspects of the animal and to develop an integrated view. This approach throws light on the current situation, for while written accounts over the centuries tell of a growing relationship between humans and cats, the biological focus sees domestication as a successful survival ploy that has been exploited by the cat.

In my book *The Wild Life of the Domestic Cat,* I concentrated on feral cats and territories, while in my BBC *Cats* book and series, I followed their historical development from earliest times to the present day. In *Understanding Cats* I take these approaches and put

them in the wider perspective of the practicalities of living with cats, from the development of kittens to the problems associated with confining cats. Yet here, too, there is an evolving story. The animal that has been thought of as both divinity and demon has retained its inheritance of independence but now in its role as pet is being increasingly restricted by fad and law. Consequently, our attitudes toward cat behavior, breeding, and care are in a state of flux.

If you perceive a cat only as an endearing creature, it can be hard to appreciate why it has brought out extremes of love and hate across the centuries. At a time when the cat has become one of the most popular animal companions in Britain and the United States, are we now in danger of attempting to redesign perfection? The cat is not just the concern of cat breeders, cat welfare organizations, or pet food manufacturers, but of us all. Yet our close

relationship with the cat as a household pet in its present widespread scale is only of recent origin. I hope that by displaying the merits of the cat in this book, I can contribute toward a greater appreciation and understanding of cats, those most enigmatic and wonderful of animals.

Origins – from wild to domestic

When your cat looks at you, it can convey the essence of contentment and trust, yet a second glance can reflect a little of the wildness that mirrors the rest of the family. For its size, its range of weapons are as formidable as those of the tiger. As hunters, the cat family is unsurpassed. Despite domestic living, our pet cats have retained many features of their wild ancestry. This apparent contradiction makes our cats the most truly enigmatic of animals. The cat retains an independence that is treasured by all true cat lovers.

It is intriguing that the two animals that most closely share our lives as pets today, the cat and dog, are both carnivores and hunters. Yet while the dog was one of the first domesticated animals, the cat was one of the last.

This was not by chance but a consequence of the differing lifestyles of the animals and our lifestyle at the time. Our activities as herd hunters overlapped those of the wolf packs, and their ability to scavenge allowed them to haunt mankind's camps. The rest is history.

It took our dramatic lifestyle and landscape changes over thousands of years to domesticate the cat. The development of agriculture and subsequent settlement and urbanization that arose from agricultural surpluses produced the waste that provided scavengeable material in sufficient abundance to support a population of normally lone-hunting cats. When we see feral or gone-wild cats scavenging to survive, we are watching a replay of the events that drew the cat into our lives. The move by the cat into domestic living has been a survival ploy that has worked spectacularly. While originally the cat had only a local distribution in the Middle East, it is now worldwide in huge numbers.

Both cats and dogs have had a working relationship with us for most of their history. The status that most household cats hold as pets today is a very recent role. We are still adjusting to that changed role. Its significance should not be underestimated, for the numbers and distribution of all other cat species are in decline because of habitat destruction and conflict with humans.

It has been during the period that the domestic cat moved into predominantly pet status that the decline of wild cats has been so dramatic. From the mid-

19th century, mankind's own numbers and destruction of huge areas of virgin planet surface have exploded exponentially. As man thrived, so did the domestic cat, as a result of the massive increase in food supply for both house and feral animals.

How Did It All Begin?

Ancestors of the mammalian families of today began to emerge during the reign of the dinosaurs. Their temperature control allowed them to move at night and to survive cooler conditions than reptiles could. Developing from these 60 million years ago, the Miacids, a

group of forest-dwelling flesh-eaters, flourished, which gave rise to all the groups of today's carnivorous mammals. Around 50 million years ago Dinictis, an early form of cat about the size of a lynx, emerged, and today's cats developed from it. The first big group of Felidae to become established were the saber-toothed cats around 34 million years ago, when many large mammals developed as the climate cooled. At first sight, the saber-toothed cats seem a crazy spur for evolution to have taken, for surely those enormous teeth would have been a great hindrance to eating by blocking the

Feral cats scavenge in a rubbish bin in Spain. In urban areas scavenging is more productive for feral cat survival than hunting.

Compare the skull of a modern tiger (foreground) with that of a saber-toothed cat, smilodon. The length of the tiger's stabbing teeth of the lower and upper jaws combined is similar to that of the saber-tooth.

Opposite: The cheetah has proportionally the smallest canines among cats.

mouth. However, they are one of the cat's great success stories, for the saber-tooth was the dominant type of cat from the Miocene to the end of the Pliocene Epoch. Some saber-toothed cats were still around only 13,000 years ago, so they survived as a subfamily for nearly 34 million years. In contrast, many modern cats and mankind have been around for a brief time.

The spread of grass landscapes around 25 million years ago encouraged huge grazing herds, benefiting the lion-sized smilodon, the biggest saber-toothed cat. Smilodon could not use the asphyxiating neck bite or the modern cat's neck bite with open mouth, but it could stab prey to kill it.

The line that gave rise to our present cats developed around 15 million years ago. The demise of the cooperatively hunting saber-toothed cats happened with the extinction of their large ungulate prey 10,000 years ago. The dominant role of the saber-toothed cats for such a long period in the development of the cat family

underlies the absurdity of calling the big fangs of the cat "canines." On any species of modern cat, even without the saber-tooths, these teeth are far larger than in the dog family. They really should be "felines."

The Modern Cat Develops

Today's cats both big and small, although having large canine teeth in the upper jaw, also have a pair of near-matching "daggers" in the lower jaw.

Biochemical sampling shows that the South American small cats branched around 12 million years ago in the cat family tree. About 9 million years ago the ancestors of the small cats of the Old World developed. In this analysis the great cats and the mid-sized cats (including the puma and the cheetah lines) became distinguishable around 5 million years ago, with the lynxes diverging from the great cats only 3 million years ago.

The placing of the cheetah in the pantherine lineage from the results of DNA and other biochemical data came as a surprise. The way in which its lifestyle and appearance is so highly specialized led to a belief that it must have evolved separately early on.

The cheetah is the cat farthest from the saber-tooths in having small canines to allow for the larger nasal opening that enables it to increase its air intake during a high-speed chase. However, biochemical evidence needs to be considered alongside that from paleontology and other areas. At present the cheetah's taxonomic position is still a matter for conjecture.

The Cat Family — Taxonomic Tangles

It is far from clear how many species of modern cat exist, as taxonomists continue to change what they consider is a species or subspecies with regard to certain groups of cats. The Scottish wildcat was once considered distinct from other European forest wildcats; then all of the closely related forms across not only Europe but down to the African wildcat came to be considered races of one species. Not everyone is in agreement.

This confusion is not limited to individual species but also applies to the main divisions. Most taxonomists put the majority of the big cats into *Panthera*, except the cheetah, which is put on its own in *Acinonyx*, the clouded leopard in *Neofelis*, and the small cats into *Felis*. But some put the clouded leopard into *Panthera*, while others take the marbled cat from the small cats and put it into *Pardofelis*, and put that into the *Panthera* too — and so on.

Nonbiologists usually give up trying to make sense of cat classification when they realize that the puma, which any tape measure would put into the big cats, is put into the small cats because of a tiny difference in the hyoid bones and larynx in its throat.

R. F. Ewer, just 20 years ago, could write, "The nomenclature of the Felidae presents a major problem, and almost the only point on which there is universal agreement is that the Cheetah requires a genus of its own." Even that is disputed now.

The Siberian tiger is the largest of the modern cats.

However, the ocelot, margay, tiger cat, and Geoffroy's cat are all bracketed into the subgenus *Leopardus* because they have 36 chromosomes rather than the 38 of most cats, including the domestic cat.

CATS IN CRISIS

The days of big animals in the wild are numbered, the days of big carnivores more so, and those of the solitary hunting forest cats particularly. The reason is simple — they require huge areas for home ranges in which to hunt. Even without other pressures, such continuous habitat is becoming increasingly fragmented and destroyed.

The immediate story of the big cats over the next 30 years will be the contrast between those requiring specific habitat, like the tiger and jaguar, and the generalists, such as the leopard and the puma. The specialists that require forest habitat are doomed in comparison to the generalists, which will probably survive, though at lower levels than today. The specialists will remain only in zoos or be sustained with great effort in special specimen reserves.

The Great Cats' Survival — The Tiger Test Case

Officially the tiger has been saved, but unofficially its collapse is inevitable. It has been brought back from the brink of destruction mainly by the actions of Project Tiger, involving the World Wide Fund for Nature, the International Union for Conservation of Nature, and various governments, particularly that of India.

During the 19th and 20th centuries, shooting parties made up of maharajas and the British Raj, followed by a ruthless postindependence agricultural policy, drastically reduced the entire tiger population of India to fewer than 2,000 by the end of the 1960s. Worldwide, only 5,000 tigers remained, when just 40 years earlier there had been more than 100,000. Firearms, agricultural poisons, and habitat loss by massive deforestation across Asia eradicated 95 percent of tigers in half a lifetime.

The situation is worse than is usually realized, for entire races of tiger are already gone. There were eight races, but in 1937 the Balinese became extinct, followed more recently by the Javanese. Both the Chinese and Russian governments attempted to exterminate entire tiger populations in the name of agricultural productivity. Forest clearance and direct tiger killing by the Russian army probably sent the Caspian tiger to extinction. China's extermination policy almost eradicated the Chinese tiger, but fortunately in 1979 official policy changed to protect it. The effects of war in Laos, Cambodia, and Vietnam and military rule in Burma have been disastrous for tiger populations. The

Siberian tiger has been badly mauled for the Far East medical trade.

In countries like India the response to dwindling numbers has been magnificent. Tiger reserves have been set aside, and numbers have increased. Yet the key problem remains that in India most tigers are in small isolated populations doomed not to survive.

What is needed is an adequate gene flow, which will require close monitoring and coordination. Due to the active-breeding sex ratios, it is the male lines that are restrictive. Moving adult and subadult tigers around would create behavioral and territorial

problems. Capture and release of the animals, plus artificial reproduction techniques, would be more likely to succeed. The use of semen, eggs, and embryos from zoo animals may be of the greatest benefit — provided that the tiger races and original areas of the animals are known.

Species-survival computer programs are currently employed in zoos for big cat pairings to ensure that races survive in captivity. While simple artificial insemination in wild cats has physiological problems, both embryo transfer and in-vitro fertilization offer more promise to isolated wild

This Bengal tiger in north India is confident that its camouflage markings blend it perfectly into its tropical surroundings of tall grasses, but such wild habitat is disappearing fast.

populations. These techniques were first used successfully on the domestic cat in 1988, and since then they have been used on tigers and other wild cats in zoos. The next step is to support tigers in the wild. These artificial reproduction techniques could prevent the genetic collapse of not only the tiger but also other endangered cats.

Other Big Cats

Loss of distribution range plus loss of numbers has been a consistent feature for cats in modern times.

Most people believe that the lion, as "King of the Beasts," is secure, but few monarchies are secure today. Seven races or subspecies of lion have been recognized, but the last southern Cape lion was shot in 1865, and the northern Barbary lion became extinct in 1922. Until recent historic times lions ranged across Africa and throughout the Middle East and north India. However, the

introduction of firearms shredded these populations, so that by World War I only 20 lions remained in India's Gir Forest. Although these have increased since then, their low ebb led to fertility problems.

Like the lion, the cheetah had a range encompassing India as well as Africa, but the last three Indian males were shot in 1948. The cheetah cannot cope with habitat changes, and between 1955 and 1970 the world population halved. Due to population losses in the past from which the cheetah recovered, their genetic base is narrow, making them susceptible to disease.

The jaguar once ranged across the Southwest of the United States and throughout Central and South America. Now its only stronghold is in the Amazon Basin, and forest destruction has put it under pressure.

The huge international trade in wild cat skins, in particular those of the spotted cats, has been massively reduced by the CITES agreement, but the trade still flourishes.

The Small Cats

Not having the "pinup" status of the big cats, the small cats have a less secure future. They are featured less in zoos, so breeding programs are less established. Because they are elusive in the wild, their natural status is often unknown. We hardly know a thing about some small cats, including numbers.

For example, very little is known about the kodkod, the Andean mountain cat, or the Borneo Bay cat. We know little of the oncilla, apart from

The Pampas cat: little is known of this distinctive South American cat's breeding patterns.

the increasing numbers killed for their skins because other spotted cats have declined. There are big gaps in our knowledge of the flat-headed cat, the Pampas cat, the rusty spotted cat, and even the clouded leopard. The Chinese desert cat does not live in deserts; it is still unclear what type of cat is the iriomote; and what is the onza? It is likely that a number of these cats will pass into oblivion without our knowledge of their lives improving very much unless supreme efforts are made.

Fortunately, not all small wild cats are in the same situation, but that does not make them secure. The main ancestor of the domestic cat, the forest wildcat (*Felis silvestris*), has a range that encompasses Britain, Europe, and a large part of Asia and, in the form of the African wildcat (*Felis silvestris lybica*), takes in much of Africa. Agricultural changes, woodland loss, and persecution in Britain and Europe have robbed it of much of its distribution.

THE EGYPTIAN ORIGINS OF THE DOMESTIC CAT

The nearest living relatives of the first domestic cats can be seen in the colorful surroundings of the centuries-old Khan el Khalili bazaar in Cairo.

These lithe, self-sufficient cats that silently patrol the ancient alleyways are direct descendants of the first of their kind. They are fed by shopkeepers, who continue a long tradition of benevolent attention to street cats in the city.

The domestic cat was a species born into this world with the status of a god. This was not just recognition of the

"otherworldly" character of the small cat but the result of its identification with its larger cousins.

From earliest times in ancient Egypt, a link existed between the sun's searing heat and the aggressive power of the lion. The lion-bodied Sphinx guards the pyramids at Giza and faces due east to meet the sun's first rays. The pharaohs Cheops and Chephren, who built these pyramids, also built the earliest part of the temple of the cat goddess Bastet at the ancient city of Bubastis in the Nile Delta around 4,500 years ago. It was then dedicated to a lion-headed Bastet, similar in appearance to Sakhmet. Bastet's link was with productive warmth, while Sakhmet's was with desiccating heat. When the small cat became domesticated, bronzes and carvings of Bastet began to be made as a small cat or as a cat-headed woman. Bastet was a local deity until a Libyan chieftain who had made Bubastis his base seized the throne of Egypt. He made his city the capital, and its

The fishing cat is endangered in parts of its range. It lives in wetlands, where it scoops fish out of the water and even dives after them.

A bronze mask of an ancient Egyptian cat mummy.

goddess took national prominence. In this city of cats, the goddess's temple was built of finely worked granite, but today not one stone remains standing upon another.

Herodotus, who visited Bastet's temple in the fifth century B.C., when the cult of the cat was at its height, recorded that the temple provided the site for the chief annual assembly for a god. Over 700,000 people made the pilgrimage, which must have been the bulk of the country's population.

It is worthwhile trying to visualize the scale of events and their importance to the participants, for archeologists have invariably marginalized the importance of the cat, preferring the lure of excavations of the pharaohs. Yet to contemporaries, the cat goddess was the key female fertility deity, on an equal footing with the Greek Artemis or the Roman Diana. Millions of cats were mummified and buried at the extensive cat cemeteries of Bubastis and at other cat cult centers.

We know from Herodotus's own words that the festival dedicated to the cat was celebrated "with abundant sacrifices," and X-rays have shown that a number of cats had their necks broken. Yet when a cat died naturally, householders shaved off their own eyebrows in remorse and carried their cat to Bubastis for embalming and burial. This apparent contradiction of sentiment is not unusual, for most religions held an element of ritual sacrifice of an aspect of the deity.

Despite the huge deposit of material that remained buried intact for more

than 3,500 years after domestication, most mummified cats were discovered and mined out in the 19th century. After a handful of the grander cat mummies reached the main museums of Europe, their economic value fell. Most ended up as fertilizer, and shipments even reached Britain for this purpose. After this storehouse of information had been kept for centuries, before we could work out the true origins of the domestic cat, the material was

Top: A seated cat, as Bastet, was chiseled in sheet gold on Tutankhamen's funerary case.

Above: The mummified head of a mature adult cat still retains its skin and some hair, from Pakhet's Temple. The skull of a modern cat lies behind it.

Opposite: This street cat in the Khan el Khalili bazaar, Cairo, is identical to the first domestic cats. There is a centuries-old tradition of feeding these stray cats in the city.

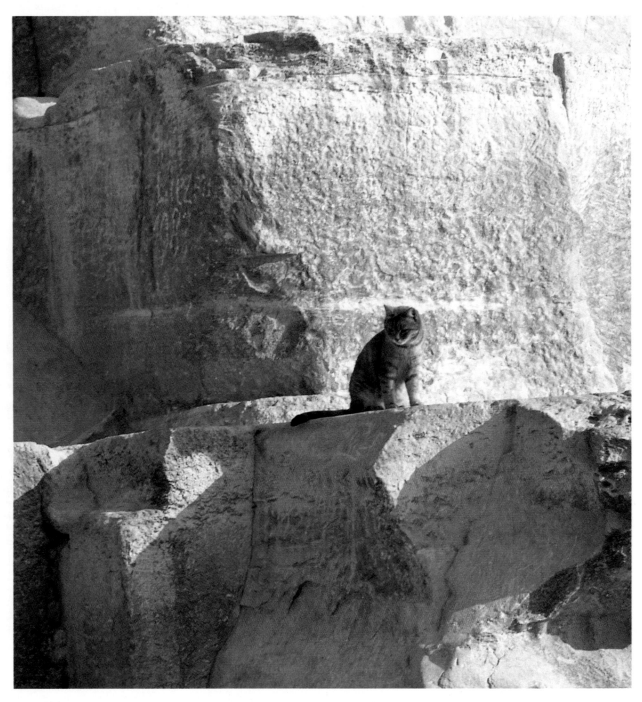

A feral cat is shown on one of the limestone blocks that make up the Great Pyramid at Giza, Egypt.

Opposite above: The African wildcat is the main ancestor of the domestic cat.

Opposite below: The marsh cat is more tractable than the African wildcat.

destroyed. Due to the importance of finding the origin of the domestic cat, I pursued it in Egypt.

While Bastet's city has been encroached upon by the spreading urban sprawl of modern Zagazig, the rock-carved Temple of Pakhet, the cat goddess of Middle Egypt, remains isolated. The earliest domesticated cats

once walked in its carved-out rooms, and it may be where a significant part of the story of the cat's domestication took place.

While it has been held that the only ancestor of the domestic cat was the African wildcat (*Felis lybica*), I believe I was the first to identify the marsh (or jungle) cat (*Felis chaus*) in one of the earliest cat paintings in Egypt, in Khnumhotep's tomb, close to the temple. It is most unlikely that the artist could have made such a sensitive portrait of this elusive animal without the familiarity gained from its captivity. In the temple's Ptolemaic extension, I found bones of the marsh cat, showing it had been kept captive alongside the African wildcat.

It is quite possible that domestication took place just by more tractable individuals of the African wildcat exploiting the scavengeable wastes of the developing towns. Yet the confining of the two species of wildcat in close captivity would undoubtedly have produced hybrids, and that may have been critical in the initial stages of the domestication story.

Amazingly, during the filming of my BBC TV series *Cats* at Pakhet's Temple, I discovered only the second ancient Egyptian cat cemetery to be found this century. It was thought that the area had been completely mined out in the 19th century, and on my previous searches I had found only a scattering of bones. But as we started filming, I suddenly realized that overnight a 9-inch seam of cat mummies had become visible as a result of movement on a slope of loose material fronting the temple area.

All along the 200-foot seam, skulls and bones protruded, there were limbs still covered with fur, and bandages brown with age. From this site, where both marsh and African wildcats were kept, it may at last be possible to work out the origin of the domestic cat.

The best-bred cat – the moggie

A mackerel tabby in Turkey has the slim form found around the Mediterranean: the original moggie.

Opposite: For centuries the cat was a working animal, controlling rodents, rather than a pet. This English tabby, seen hunting in an old water mill, still has the original spotted mackerel pattern, but it is of "cobby" northern build.

Moggies, as British cat lovers call non-purebred cats (see box on facing page), are good, gutsy animals that have the best possible pedigree, going back unhindered through the mists of time. Because of their near-random mating, they have enjoyed the best possible breeding program for countless generations. Their survival and subsequent breeding derived from natural selection, favoring functioning characteristics. It is an unbeatable combination for healthy animals, producing a natural perfection of design and function.

Far more people live with moggies than with breed cats — 90 percent are moggies — yet picture editors are not alone in liking to see variety on their pages.

The high-profile events that promote cats — the major cat shows — primarily promote breeds and breeding rather than moggies and the selection of good pets. Of course, breed cats can and do make good pets, but as millions of people will testify, so do moggies.

I admit to a bias, because my cats are moggies. I choose to have moggies because I believe they are proper cats, the essence of cat and not genetically messed with. Among cat writers this must put me into a fairly serious minority, for traditionally most writers have been breeders, with a bias not only toward breeds but toward their special breed. My approach as a cat biologist and behaviorist is fundamentally to look at this incredibly successful species that shares our lives, and find out what makes it tick — to try to understand the cat.

Moggies on average live much longer than breed cats because they are genetically more robust. In recent years breed cats seem to be reaching better ages than previously, but usually with significant veterinary attention.

In the real world the majority of cats are moggies, with purebred cats just a tiny minority. In geographically isolated areas historic breeds have developed naturally, unaffected by cross-breeding with another type, and in some countries the whole local moggie population is made up of the original cats of a fancy breed, such as the Angora in Anatolia, the Siamese and Korat in Thailand, and the Japanese Bobtail in Japan (it took the occupying Americans after World War II to point out that the Bobtail was special). In the same way it is easy to underrate the real British, European, and American Shorthair on the streets, for to us it is just a moggie.

STRIPES AND SPOTS

In its journey north from Egypt, the domestic cat entered the realm of the European forest cat. Just as today the Scottish wildcat is hybridizing with feral domestic cats, so when any of the new domestic animals became lost and turned feral, they would have mated with wild cats. It is hard to believe that the stockier build of the British and European moggie came into existence any other way, although it could have happened by mutation. Compared to the markings of its African ancestors, the bolder markings of the moggie are consistent with such hybridizing. The original slim, paler cats are still to be

WHAT IS A "MOGGIE"?

America, which has made an art form of slang, does not seem to have an accepted word for the non-pedigree cat, the "average Joe" of the cat world. Terms used such as *alley cat*, *common cat* and *tabby* all have other meanings, and none conveys the exactness of the affectionate British slang word "moggie," which is worth introducing to Americans.

The classic tabby cat is darker than the striped form and so was able to merge safely into the shadows of European towns during the witchcraft era.

found around the Mediterranean basin, where the climate suits their build and they remain as the southern street moggie. Among the early Egyptian cats were both fine-striped and spotted tabbies, and they are still there.

As there is a gradation in tabby markings of striped into spotted, the cat geneticist Roy Robinson has suggested that instead of the spotted and mackerel tabbies being from different genes, it is more likely that they are one type modified by polygenes (see p. 48). While this is probably the case, I think this part of their inheritance occurred before domestication, for the African wildcat has both a spotted and striped form, and Egypt is located centrally to their ranges. The genetic reinforcement by the domestic cat hybridizing with the wild spotted Eastern variety when it was taken to India may well have caused the preponderance of beautiful blue-silver spotted tabbies in Nepal.

Tabby Types

All cats are genetically tabbies, even if they do not look like it. Even a black-and-white cat carries tabby genes. There are four types of tabby patterns: the classic tabby, mackerel tabby, spotted tabby, and agouti tabby.

In early medieval Europe a new type of tabby appeared — the classic tabby. Instead of the pattern of narrow parallel bands seen in the mackerel tabby, the new mutation had blobs and swirls. The new tabby spread around the world, carried on ships traveling to various parts of the growing British Empire, and so a number of years ago I dubbed the humble classic tabby "the British Imperial Cat." The classic tabby not only has reached as far as Hong Kong and Australia but is also surviving in the freezing conditions of subantarctic islands alongside penguins.

Only in recent years has it been possible to trace the spread of marking and coat color mutations as researchers in different countries pool their observations to draw up gene-frequency maps. These show the distribution not so much of the type of cat (the phenotype) as of the mutated gene itself (the allele). In 1977 Neil Todd, by plotting the frequencies for the allele for the classic tabby, found that the initial waves of settlers sailing from Britain to America in the 17th century, Canada in the 18th century, and Australia in the 19th century took increasing numbers of classic tabbies among their cats as each century passed. This happened as the proportion of classic tabbies increased in Britain. Their increase probably occurred because the classic tabby has a darker coat than the mackerel tabby. From medieval times until the 19th century, landlubbers, unlike sailors, had little time for cats. Consequently, the patterned coat of the classic tabby was a decided aid to survival in the murky

shadows of a town street. Most cats then lived alongside us rather than with us.

Tabbies come in a fascinating range of colors; among them are cream, brown, blue, red, chocolate, lilac, cameo and golden.

Sailors had a high regard for cats because their own survival could depend on them. Rats and mice on board ship could ruin a cargo, destroy the food supply, and even endanger the ship. So while the oceans have stopped the spread of many animals, they have assisted the distribution of the cat, with a little help from man.

From the distribution of the classic tabby mutation, Britain still holds the highest density of these cats, and working back from present-day figures, it probably occurred around A.D. 1200.

One major type of tabby, the agouti, or Abyssinian type, is rarely thought of

HYBRIDIZING WITH WILDCATS

During medieval times the forest wildcat (*Felis silvestris*) was hunted for sport and for its fur, as was the feral domestic cat. It was lost from southern England probably by the 16th century. By World War I it had retreated virtually to the Scottish Highlands. Its eradication from England was largely due to deforestation, a habitat change that better suited the feral-living domestic cat. In Scotland gamekeeping on shooting estates was more responsible. When this ceased after World War I, the Scottish wildcat seemed to recover very quickly and expanded into the Lowlands.

Yet when skulls were examined, the average Scottish wildcat was said to be only 66 percent wildcat because of hybridizing with feral domestic cats. This has also been found across Europe, with an average of 63 percent. Since the European wildcat across Europe is noticeably smaller than in Neolithic times, this could suggest that there was a long period of hybridizing from when the domestic cat began its expansion.

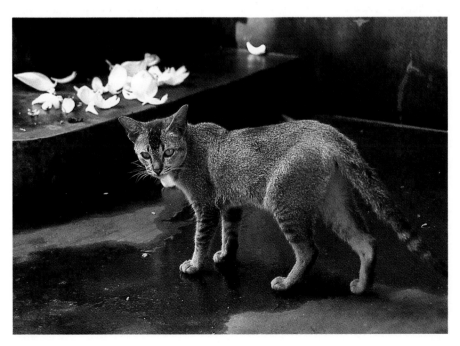

A feral street agouti-patterned tabby in Bangkok, Thailand, shows the leg and face patterns that breeders of Abyssinians try to avoid.

by most people as a tabby at all, mainly because it lacks stripes. However, even in the breed form, there are tabby markings on the forehead, face, and tail.

Breeders have worked hard to reduce these markings, and a street agouti tabby has far clearer face and forehead patterning.

The show Abyssinian's beautiful cinnamon agouti coat, with its "natural shadowing," has the same natural shadowing of the jungle cat. It makes Abyssinian kittens perhaps the prettiest of all. Devotees suggest that it has been around since the time of the ancient Egyptians. It is arguable that some of the Egyptian statues show agouti-marked cats, but these could well be jungle cats that were kept captive on temple sites.

Abyssinian kittens sit with a bronze statue of Bastet. The clear tabby markings on the kittens' foreheads fade as they become adult.

Opposite: The Maine Coon was a moggie that became America's most notable native breed cat; it developed as a rugged long-haired farm cat able to survive harsh New England winters.

A ginger tabby parks on double yellow lines.

I have found most agouti-marked domestic cats to be in Southeast Asia, usually with gray-looking agouti coats.

Other Tabby Colors

The distribution of the gene of the ginger cat indicates that its original mutation occurred in Turkey centuries ago and was carried north by Viking traders, who liked the cat's unusual color. Traveling by rivers, they took the cat to the Baltic from Byzantium via the Black Sea. The ginger toms found on Scottish islands and in Ireland are living relatives of the cats that lived in Viking settlements.

While the basic tabby has black as its dark marking, the flecked section varies from yellow to tan and full brown. This variability is believed to be due to polygenes. A fine ginger tom is still a tabby, even though the black markings have been replaced by orange ones. True tabby markings can be found under such guises as cinnamon, blue, and silver colorings — and not just among fancy cats.

The Black Cat — The First of the Solid Colors

Gene frequencies suggest that the initial spread of the black cat, one of the earliest mutations, was aided by Phoenician shipping. Active traders around the Mediterranean were operating at a time when very few cats had been allowed out of Egypt. The adherents of the fertility cult of the cat goddess Bastet actively sought to confine them within their country. As it left Egypt, the cat began to change from god to mog.

From altar to show bench

When the black cat arrived in Europe, it was accepted as a working cat. But as the centuries passed, it was destined to become synonymous with the Prince of Darkness.

THE FEMININE FELINE

Soft and *sensuous* are descriptive words that can be applied as equally to a cat as to a woman. A fable credited to Aesop tells how a man fell in love with his cat, which Venus, in compassion, changed into a beautiful woman; however, when a mouse ran by their bed, she leaped out onto it, changing back into a cat. So readily interchangeable are feline and feminine in our minds that in advertisements an elegant cat will be shown alongside an equally elegant woman to convey a sexy image.

There has been a long-held association of dog and man, and

woman and cat. Fundamentally, it may just reflect the historic role of the sexes and the associated role of these animals; men as hunters went out accompanied by their dogs of the chase, while women worked around the homestead, where the cat slept beside the fire and stalked mice in the yard.

Before the rise of Christianity, all the religions across Europe had a mother earth goddess figure who was held as a fount of fertility while being eternally virginal. For the Greeks it was Artemis, for the Romans, Diana, and for the Scandinavians, Freyja. The Egyptian goddess Bastet was associated with fertility in women, as well as warmth, love, dance, and the moon. When the Greek Ptolemy became pharaoh, he had inscriptions carved on the cat rock temple near Beni Hasan, which he called Speos Artemedos — Temple of Artemis.

Diana was a moon goddess, living in celibacy and presiding over women, as did Bastet. So, not surprisingly, when Typhon waged war on the gods, Diana escaped — by turning into a cat. In London, St. Paul's was built on the site of a cult shrine to Diana. A sistrum has also been excavated in London that was used in the worship of the Egyptian fertility goddesses, including Bastet. It is an intriguing thought that worship of the cat goddess Bastet may have taken place with that of Diana on the site of St. Paul's in Roman Londinium.

Despite the best endeavors of the Egyptians, not only did the reputation of cats leak out of Egypt, but so did some of the animals. Illustrations of domestic cats first began turning up in Italy around the fourth and fifth centuries B.C. When Christianity was made the Roman state religion in the fourth century A.D., other religions such as the following of Bastet were banned.

In Egypt the main cat divinity was Bastet, whose chief center of worship was in the city of Bubastis. At the massive annual pilgrimage each year, thousands of devotees, mainly women, sang, danced, drank, and shook sistrums.

The ancient Egyptians noted that the size of the pupil of the cat's eyes varied with the phase of the moon. Although this is caused simply by the amount of prevailing light, it was thought to be magical. Because a woman's cycle has a monthly periodicity, it was logical to recognize the links between women, cats, and the moon.

The cat goddess's fertility role for women is revealed in tomb wall paintings found near Luxor. In scenes of domesticity husband and wife are

Above: Bastet in the form of a cat-headed woman is shown with four kittens at her feet and shaking a sistrum, symbolic of her role as fertility goddess.

Below: Egyptian ladies and girls hold a litter of kittens born in the site excavations at Bubastis, the cult center of women's fertility dedicated to the cat goddess Bastet.

portrayed as they hoped to be in their afterlifes. When a cat is shown with them, it is always under the seat of the woman. The cat as an incarnation of the goddess was positioned to enhance the wife's afterlife fertility.

Although the Egyptians' regard for their cats diminished with the passage of time, in Europe the historic link between cats and women persisted and indeed has lasted until the present day.

THE CAT MOVES NORTH TO BRITAIN

The Phoenicians could have introduced the cat to Britain, but while Himilco of Carthage may have landed on an exploratory voyage around 425 B.C., evidence of any direct trade is lacking.

Unambiguous evidence of a domestic cat appears in Camulodunum (Colchester), the main "city" of Celtic Britain just before the Roman invasion. A cat bone found alongside domestic stock is strong evidence of the domestic animal. I like to think it was a diplomatic gift to the old "king of Britain," whom the Roman authorities had been "keeping sweet." When he died, they invaded.

Abundant domestic cat remains have been excavated from several Roman fort and villa sites, often found in wells that had been used for rituals.

The Cat in Ireland

Once the cat had reached England, it is likely that it arrived in Ireland as a consequence of trade. Excavations show not only that the domestic cat was widespread in monastic sites across

Ireland during the early Christian era but that it was enjoying a contented life, as revealed by a contemporary monk's poem about his feline companion, Pangur Ban. These cats reached a good age.

In contrast, excavations on Viking and medieval towns have shown that although cats reached adulthood, most died young. The same young age pattern has been found in some English medieval cities. Cat skulls from medieval York and from an Irish site show knife marks around the orbits, which is evidence of skinning. Pelts of all sorts, including the cat's, were an important part of medieval trade.

The cat's role changed from contemplative companion to utilitarian commodity. As its numbers increased with the increase in the size of towns, its rarity value declined. In 1358 Edward III bestowed a murage grant of a halfpenny on the port of Youghal in Ireland for the exportation of each 100 cat pelts.

The Witches' Cat

When one religion usurps another, the deities of the old faith are relegated to the position of demons. When Christianity replaced the older religions, followers of the fertility deities were deemed heretical. Time amalgamated beliefs, and followers of the old fertility rituals were hounded as witches.

The woodland hunting biology of this new animal to Europe was not understood by medieval people any more than it was by the ancient Egyptians, but while shining, reflective eyes helped make the cat a goddess to

VIKING FURS

Evidence that the Vikings used the pelts of the domestic cat in their everyday lives is revealed by the skinner's pit excavated at Odense, Denmark. Dating from A.D. 1070, it contained the remains of at least 68 cats. The cats had been killed by a sudden wrench of the head and had skinning cut marks. Most of the cats were about 10 or 11 months old, so their coats would have been adult size but undamaged. This led Tove Hatting to suggest that they had been bred in captivity to provide fur. The remains of the fully grown adults were of animals slighter than the Danish moggies of today, which is consistent with the arrival of the lighter-built eastern Mediterranean cats via Viking trade at an early date.

Opposite: Initially the cat was accepted by the church in Europe, but this attitude changed as the cat became identified with the devil.

the Egyptians, they reinforced its damnable identity in Europe.

From witchcraft trial documents, it is apparent that in Britain the cat as familiar was thought to be central to witchcraft. To accusers a cat could be an agent of the devil or the devil himself. They believed that the wishes of a witch were enacted by the demonic cat familiar against her neighbors.

The first major witchcraft trial in England took place in Chelmsford, Essex, in 1565 and set the pattern for later trials. It revolved around the ownership of a cat that was dangerously called Satan by three women. An original report of the trial survives in Lambeth Palace Library. The accusers thought that the women suckled the cat with blood from unnatural teats. It became routine to search an accused woman for a "teat," and a wart was considered damning evidence. From the trial records, neither the women nor their accusers believed that the women had had any supernatural power until they obtained the cat.

Only a few enlightened independent-minded people led the vanguard of the cat's acceptance, but the country that showed the way was France. Although cats were still being burned alive in street bonfire festivals in the 17th century, they became fashionable among French aristocrats at the court of Louis XIV. The leading lady poet at the court, Madame Deshoulières, wrote poetic love letters on behalf of her cat Grisette to the cats of her friends, and they replied in like manner. This was remarkable, for in the era of witchcraft persecution, from

The light-reflective eyes of the nocturnal hunting cat were misinterpreted as magical by ancient Egyptians and medieval to 18th-century Europeans.

the mid-16th century to the end of the 17th, ownership of a cat could result in a death sentence.

Even in the early 18th century, in Caithness the link between cats and witches was still strong enough for the deaths of two elderly women and the injury to another's leg to be attributed to the actions of a man who had attacked a group of caterwauling cats with an ax the night before.

As "witches" found, the identification of women with cats is not always kind. Women are accused of being "catty," but not men. Yet this is not new, for in the 18th century a common name for a prostitute was "cat."

CATS AND WEATHER PREDICTION

From all ages and all around the world, the ability of the cat to anticipate

Opposite: For centuries, across Britain and Europe, cats were burned alive in wicker baskets, suspended above the flames to prolong their agony, as it was believed that this hurt the devil (a reconstruction for the BBC TV series Cats).

Girls dress up as cats at the annual Ypres Cat Festival in Belgium, demonstrating the interchangeability of feminine and feline.

changes in the weather has been recorded. Mariners have known that when a cat becomes skittish, "it has the wind up its tail."

A major reason for the official vindictive attitude toward witches in 17th-century Britain stems from the severe storm that almost wrecked the ship on which James VI of Scotland was returning from Scandinavia with his new wife, Queen Anne. Alleged witches claimed to have instigated the storm. James became outraged when one of the witches was acquitted, and he took over the running of the trial. The women "confessed" that they had conjured the storm by roping bits cut from a dead man to a cat, which was then thrown into the sea. The King then spent years writing his book *Demonology,* which was published in 1597. When he was made James I of England, he published a new edition

and instigated a draconian new witchcraft law.

James did not doubt the power of witches over weather. Unfortunately for the cat, it could be demonstrated that they could foretell the weather. The cat is particularly attributed with anticipating rain, though fortunately today we realize that this is not the same as causing it.

Robert Herrick, the English poet, was just six years old when James's book was first published. Herrick lived in isolation in a Devon vicarage, where he came to delight in the continuity of pre-Christian rural customs. In his peaceful seclusion cats were Herrick's main companions, and they confirmed for him the traditional belief that cats could predict the weather:

True calendars as Pusse's eare,
Wash't o're to tell what change is neare.

With such interests, it is small wonder that when the Puritans came to power, they threw Herrick out of his living.

In 1643 Herrick's contemporary, John Swan, wrote even more explicitly of the action, saying that the cat would "wash her face with her tongue; and it is observed by some that if she put her feet beyond the crown of her head in this kind of washing, it is a signe of rain."

Fortunately for the cat, at a time of antiwitch and antifeline hysteria, some kind and careful observers realized that the creatures were, in fact, passive detectors.

For 30 years I have monitored the ability of numerous cats to predict rain in this way and have yet to find an exception. It really does work. Twenty years ago I enlisted the help of viewers of BBC 1's *Animal Magic* to see if others observed the same thing and how long after the cat washed over its ear did it rain. It was found that most ear washing occurred within four hours of rain, particularly the last hour.

I have no doubt that the cat has information about changing weather; but if it interprets or acts upon that information is quite another matter. I see no reason why not. Avoiding rain can give a survival advantage at times.

I believe that the action of the cat in washing over its ear is due to humidity and pressure changes making themselves felt upon the membranes of

A cat is carved on the 16th-century windowsill of an East Anglian weaver's cottage, in the heart of witchcraft country.

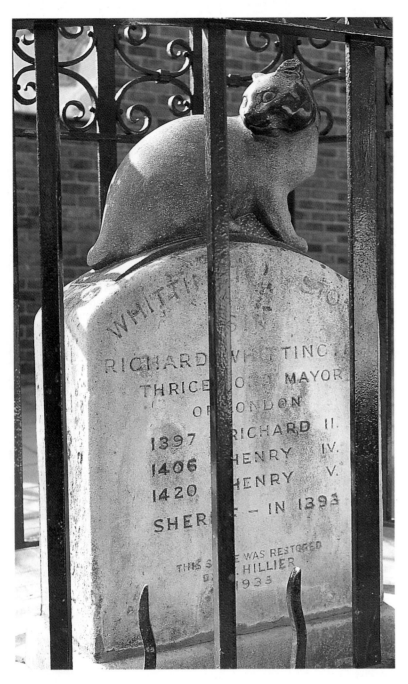

The commemorative roadside stone to Dick Whittington and his cat is located on Highgate Hill in London, where, according to tradition, he "turned again" on hearing Bow bells.

man with a huge cat cavorting on the stage beside her. It's a curiously British annual event of pantomime, when the legend of Dick Whittington and his cat has Bow bells saying "Turn again Whittington, Lord Mayor of London."

The pantomime, one of the stage's most enduring forms of entertainment, grants an intriguing view of the cat across many centuries. During the height of its popularity in the 19th century, the cat was still gaining acceptance after the evil slur of witchcraft, yet the image portrayed was often based on an earlier one of powerful magic. Pantomime helped to make cats more acceptable, assisting the change in attitude that led to the setting up of the cat fancy in 1871.

The Lord Mayor and His Cat

In the story of Dick Whittington, Dick and his cat return to London and go to sea with his merchant employer to a sultan's palace overrun by rats, which the cat kills. Dick is rewarded with a fortune and becomes Lord Mayor. Sir Richard Whittington really was Lord Mayor in 1397, 1406, and 1419, and he did make a fortune — but how?

The pantomime derives from a play in the mold of the tales of French magic cats, in which the cat aids its master with good fortune. Puss-in-Boots, also written down in the 17th century from traditional tales, has a poor youth made rich by his cunning cat, which tricks an ogre into turning into a mouse. Having a cat for good luck was not passive but in some way thought to cause the luck, but there is no evidence that Richard Whittington ever owned one.

the inner ear and eardrum. It must feel something like the air pressure changes we humans undergo on takeoff and landing in a plane.

THE WORLDLY STAGE OF PANTOMIME CATS

In Britain at Christmastime generations of children have witnessed the sight of a young woman dressed as a young

What of the rats in the legend? Dick was born 10 years after the Black Death had wiped out half the population of London. At the time the link between rats and disease was not known, but the black rat population was enormous and the cat's controlling role was understood. Belief in the cat's magical powers led to the creature's interment in house walls to keep rats and evil away.

Similar stories to Dick's exist — back to a 10th-century tale from Persia — suggesting that the legend was grafted to his name once he had been linked to sudden good fortune and a cat. Amazingly, as in the pantomime, Dick really married Alice, the merchant's daughter. The medieval sense of humor may have been at work on the Lord Mayor, for a clue lies in the two last lines that were inscribed as a memorial on his tomb:

For lo! he scorned to gain by stealth
What he got by a cat.

Dick gained a specific fortune by a cat rather than stealing it. The "cat" was Alice, and when he married her, he suddenly became much richer. *Cat* was a common term for a spiteful woman. The old expression "to live under a cat's foot" described a henpecked man. Dick may have married his "cat" for "good fortune" and needed a bit of magic for that match. The tales of Dick Whittington, Puss-in-Boots, and others are the positive side of "cat magic" seen by the perpetrators rather than the persecutors.

The White Cat

A very popular 19th-century pantomime that has almost disappeared without a trace was *The White Cat*. The heroine, a cat-headed woman, looked remarkably like the cat goddess Bastet. A king's three sons had to fulfill tasks to inherit the crown. The youngest became entranced by the White Cat, who magically helped him. Having succeeded in the first two tasks, the sons pursued the third task, which was to return with the most beautiful princess. The young prince could not believe the White Cat when she instructed him to cut off her head and tail. Reluctantly he obeyed, and instantly she was transformed into a radiant princess, breaking the fairies' spell. Such woman/cat transformations worked by love have a long pedigree.

The positive portrayal of the cat in pantomime was part of the improvement in its image wrought by the literary tradition of writers and actors. The cat had powerful friends in the "PR" world, and after centuries of persecution it certainly needed them.

THE BIRTH OF THE CAT FANCY

You may loathe cat shows or you may love them, but all cat lovers owe them a debt of gratitude, for they transformed the attitude of the Western world toward cats. They were still stigmatized by the taint of witchcraft, which had left residual antipathy and antagonism toward cats.

Harrison Weir was responsible for their transformation into their position today as a supremely popular pet.

THE "FATHER OF ENGLISH PANTOMIME"

John Rich (1692–1761) began pantomime with his adaptation of Harlequinade. At a time in Britain when only the most daring people would admit to liking a cat, Rich was one of the most noted lovers of cats, with 27 of his own. The *Dublin Review* noted that an actress found him with "one licking the buttered toast on his breakfast plate, another was engaged in drinking the cream for his tea, two cats lay on one knee, one was asleep on his shoulder, and another sat demurely on his head."

The involvement of key people like Rich who doted on cats, and the arrival of pantomime's origins from lands that at the time were more pro-cat than Britain, led to the selection of positive cat-magic storylines from folktales to overlay Harlequinade. They helped to change the entrenched British ideas about the cat.

Words like *soft* and *sensuous* are used when describing both feminine and feline characteristics.

Opposite: Elegance meets elegance when a Somali cat and its owner converse at a cat show.

Renowned as the "Father of the Cat Fancy," Weir also documented its beginnings, both in his justifiably famous book *Our Cats and All About Them* and as an illustrator of cats. He had a passion for cats and was distressed at their continual shabby treatment, which he resolved to change.

Weir had a lifetime's experience as a senior judge at pigeon and poultry shows, and by bringing together his love of cats and the practical knowledge of the mechanics of showing, he established the basis of exhibiting cats. He convinced his friend Mr. Wilkinson,

manager of the Crystal Palace, that it was "a thing to be done." Weir recalled the events that followed:

"In a few days I presented my scheme in full working order: the schedule of prizes, the price of entry, the number of classes, and the points by which they would be judged, the number of prizes in each class, their amount, the different varieties of colour, form, size and sex for which they were to be given. I also made a drawing of the head of a cat to be printed black on yellow paper for a posting bill."

Cats had been exhibited as part of

agricultural shows from time to time, and cats were on display at St. Giles Fair, Winchester, in the 16th century. In that era, however, it would have been a very different exhibit. Weir's action was a watershed, for by putting 160 cats on show in the glass Crystal Palace he ensured that they were seen by a very wide audience. His first Crystal Palace show was held on July 13, 1871. The ruse worked spectacularly: cat shows became immensely popular, and the cat was soon transformed into a much-loved animal.

Weir's standards of "Points of Excellence" have been followed in essence over the years. A National Cat Club was established in 1887 as a registering body for recording cats' pedigrees. In 1910 this function was taken over by the Governing Council of the Cat Fancy (GCCF), which was formed for the purpose.

In North America, pride in the rugged farm cats of Maine had led to local shows of the breed, possibly before the first national multi-breed show launched an American cat fancy. That began when James Hyde, who had experience holding horse shows for many years at Madison Square Garden in New York, attended a Crystal Palace Cat Show while he was staying in London. On May 5, 1895, he opened the first New York show. He arranged for some eight British star cats to be shipped to New York to appear at the show to display the standards that had been achieved by showing over the quarter of a century of experience in Britain. Sadly, the temperature rose to

95°F and some of the British cats died; but others, like Topaz and The Banshee, went on to form notable dynasties.

In Britain the GCCF has been the sole arbiter of cat showing and registration for most of this century. In 1983 it was joined by an alternative organization, the Cat Association of Great Britain. In contrast, North America, due to its size, has a history of a multiplicity of registration bodies, among which is the world's largest, the Cat Fanciers Association (CFA). European countries have their own registration bodies, but these are usually linked to the Fédération Internationale Féline (FIFe).

Appropriately, the oldest national club holds Britain's National Cat Club Show. Held in December each year at Olympia (under GCCF regulations), it remains the largest event in the world, with more than 2,000 cats on show.

Still living wild

Above: Two of my Fitzroy Square colony (Diag and Double-Eye Flick) look out from their usual basement-steps sleeping area, protected by railings.

Top: Vehicles provide invaluable shelter for urban feral cats, from the cold and rain to the full heat of the sun.

Opposite: Sketches of six of the Fitzroy Square feral cats show the characteristically individual black-and-white face markings that aided identification. Their names were mainly derived from these.

The cat was one of the last animals to be domesticated, thousands of years later than the dog, and it readily reverts to living wild. The study of gone-wild, or feral, cats has taken up much of my life since I started field observations on cats in the mid-1970s.

Most people considered cats as pets only, so their very familiarity meant that the wild life of domestic cats had not been thought worth studying, even by biologists. Urban ecology was in its infancy; biologists preferred looking at "proper wildlife" in "real countryside." Research work on urban foxes led to statements that "foxes are the main predators in towns." However, I realized that house cats alone were far more numerous, and that stray and feral cats

must have an impact — but what? At that time, 20 years ago, it was thought that groups of cats were only "loose assemblages" with no social structure.

While I kept watch on a number of feral groups throughout London, my main study colony of cats was in Fitzroy Square, W1. The site was ideal for the cats, with protective railings, a large mature garden with good cover, yet also with open grass and sunning spots. The cats had a number of dedicated feeders; one in particular, Mary Wyatt, spent most of her weekly money on the cats.

It soon became clear that this was no random, varying aggregation of cats, with different animals wandering in and out. On the contrary, I observed that the same animals held the site day after day and, as the study went on, year after year. The group were all black-and-white animals — just like T. S. Eliot's "Jellicle Cats." They had certainly been in continuous residence for 20 years then and in all probability for significantly longer.

The cats were nearly all related to each other. When I started the study, a mainly white matriarch ruled the roost, although not by overt aggression. I spent night after night watching the cats, carefully monitoring their movements. As they were all black and white, I found quick sketches of their face patterns invaluable. I named them after their face patterns, which helped recognition. Sketching cats makes you look at them in a different way than when taking photographs.

When I began working with feral cats, it was standardly assumed that life for them was nasty, brutish — and short. On the contrary, however, I discovered that most feral cats were fit and robust. To check this I weighed the Fitzroy Square cats, plus those from seven other colonies, and found their weights were comparable to those of house cats. A conflicting myth to the undernourished cat was that they became monster sized by living feral, so I also measured them. Again the similarities with house cats were more noticeable than the differences.

During the 1970s I was one of a tiny handful of researchers throughout the world investigating feral cat behavior and the size of range they needed. The results of my research saw the light of day in scientific meetings and papers and in my first book, *The Wild Life of the Domestic Cat*, in the early 1980s. It was a fascinating time, for the ranges of the urban-living London feral cats I observed were smaller than those of the dockyard feral groups studied by Jane Dards in Portsmouth and much smaller than the farmyard cats monitored by David MacDonald and Peter Apps. Yet, remarkably, the pattern was the same; toms ranged wider than queens, using about 10 times the area, and the groups clumped around a source of food.

I realized that greater amounts of food resulted in more cats, for with more food available, the cats do not

have to travel so widely to find it and therefore their ranges are smaller. I was able to make a straight-line graph showing the relationship between the density at which the cats live and the size of their ranges. As time has gone on, the work of other researchers around the world has supported my conclusions — notably in 1988, when Olaf Liberg and Mikael Sandell published a similar straight-line graph using figures from studies of feral cats around the world.

Until we started to log the cats' movements, no one really had any idea of how the cats' social system of land use worked. Similar studies carried out on both tigers and forest wildcats has shown a cat family pattern of males holding significantly larger ranges than females. However, there did seem to be a difference, for while the ranges of female tigers and forest wildcats do not overlap much, the English feral cat studies showed the cats clumped around a core area that included a major food source. In Fitzroy Square it was where the feeder regularly put down food.

There are social advantages from group living, and the higher density of urban and farm feral cats, compared to wild species of cat, means it can readily occur, but is it just the result of density? The clumping of ranges seems to reflect the pockets of local abundance of food. Queens that have to catch all their food rather than scavenge from a dump or obtain food from a feeder, like those living on uninhabited islands, do not usually overlap their ranges. Yet one of

Protective Queen (female)

Diag (male)

Double-Eye Flick (female)

Black Nose (female)

Eyebrows (female)

Flat Cap (female)

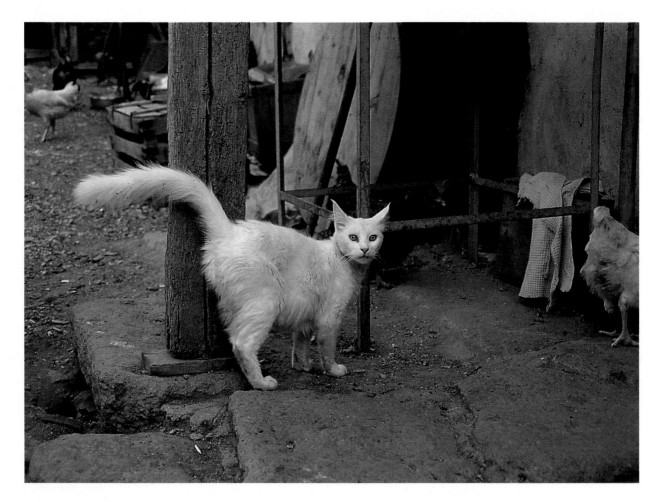

The real Angora lives in the unchanged, original hillside village of Angora, from which Ankara has developed. Despite its long hair, this cat is a working yard cat, for its coat does not tangle.

Opposite: A feral cat feeder tends to some of her cats in Venice. She is a member of the Anglo-Venetian cat welfare society Dingo.

the undoubted stars of my BBC *Cats* series was a ginger-and-white feral tom living on the Hebridean island of North Uist. Although he hunted to survive, his range did overlap with other feral cats around an abundant food source, a large rabbit warren.

So our small domestic cats, when living feral, have a flexibility over their ranges that allows them to tolerate other cats if there is a good local source of food. Yet, at the same time, they have the same basic pattern as the rest of the cat family. It is not possible to study the ranges of tigers or jaguars over such a range of food availability as it is for the domestic cat living feral, so the studies on our wild-living domestic cats have shed light on the range requirements of their larger cousins.

Around the World

I have studied cats living feral around the world and found that they live remarkably similar lives despite their radically different climates and countries. In rural areas food availability is insufficient to sustain large numbers of cats, so densities are low. There is more food to scavenge in towns, and in that, feral cats are reliving the predomestication period of the species. A significant part of the cat population is always in a feral state. In the ancient bazaars of Egypt, there are some feral cats whose lineage contains few ancestors that have known domestic life. Although that may seem remarkable, it is almost equally true in Britain. Keeping cats as pets in significant numbers is very recent, even in cat-obsessed Britain; it dates from the invention of cat shows in the 19th century and the rise of suburban living.

In Britain pet cats claim most of the country's extensive suburban landscape. To obtain food, our house cats have only to stagger from their snoozing spots to their food bowls. Consequently, feral cats cannot achieve the same density of numbers as nearby house cats do and require larger areas in which to scavenge for food. The ferals live in the gaps left by the house cats in the suburban landscape, such as hospital grounds, factories, and squares.

In many countries house cats are less common than in Britain and lead wilder lives at lower densities, as farm cats do. In reality the nearer a rural economy approaches subsistence agriculture, the more the cat remains a working animal. In a village in the Spanish Pyrenees, I recall talking to a lady about her cats. The main room of her house was her kitchen, in which chickens scratched around the floor. Her cats were rodent controllers of wild temperament. She threw them chunks of meat, over which they growled at each other. I have met the same situation in the hill villages of Turkey and the jungle villages of Nepal and many parts of the world, although the cats usually show less aggression.

Feral Cat Colony Control

The control of feral cats is an emotional issue. Traditionally in Britain, as in many countries, if an animal was regarded as a pest or problem, the automatic response was to call in someone to kill it — albeit humanely.

A reliable food source: a market's permanently sited waste dumpster in Istanbul has drawn a number of scavenging feral cats for many years; inevitably the cats in the group are now related.

In rural areas gamekeepers on estates dispatched large numbers of cats by shooting and by the barbarous and indiscriminate use of wire-noose traps and other traps. A proportion of the cats would be feral, but many were farm or house cats. Fortunately, as gamekeepers became an endangered species themselves, this practice waned.

Key places where feral colonies were thought to be a problem were large factory sites or hospitals, usually with sizable grounds. Hospital administrators thought it "self-evident" that all the cats had to be killed. However, this approach usually failed, for eradication is rarely total, and cats moved in from other areas. A controlled, stable colony prevents this "vacuum effect," as I have dubbed it. If an area is able to support a population of cats and they are eradicated, then

another group can fill its space. However, devoid of the family linkages that existed within the former group, the new cats will breed and be a less stable group.

Although a "total wipeout" often appeals to authorities because of its apparent simplicity, it normally fails, as it does not allow for biological reality, and worse, is often counterproductive. However, if a colony is neutered and returned to its area, it will continue to hold the location and keep out other cats by its presence. The group's population will gradually decline over a few years. During their brief time in captivity, veterinary inspection and treatment can ensure the good health of the group. In contrast, if they are removed from the site, other cats will move in, and being of assorted origin, will be potentially less healthy.

More than 25 years ago Celia Hammond, who abandoned her career as a top runway model and adopted the path of feral-cat caretaker, became dissatisfied with the ineffective trap-and-kill approach and began to put neutered cats back on sites. When I began monitoring my Fitzroy Square cats before and after neutering, I believe I was the first biologist to assess the effects on a feral cat group. The cats were neutered by the Cats' Protection League, and for many years after, I found that the reducing population continued to hold their area.

Paul Rees studied a hospital feral population, while Tom Kristensen of Kattens Vaern was involved in a Danish neutering-and-return scheme. In 1977 I was asked by Celia Hammond and others to launch the Cat Action Trust, which has gone on to neuter many thousands of cats all across Britain. Peter Neville monitored a site in Regent's Park with Jenny Remfry for the Universities Federation for Animal Welfare (UFAW) after Jenny had first tried and then discontinued the possible alternative of putting feral cats on the "pill."

Each of these neuter-and-return studies had similar positive findings. Subsequently the practice of neutering and returning feral cats back to their sites has been applied widely by organizations, including the World Society for the Protection of Animals in

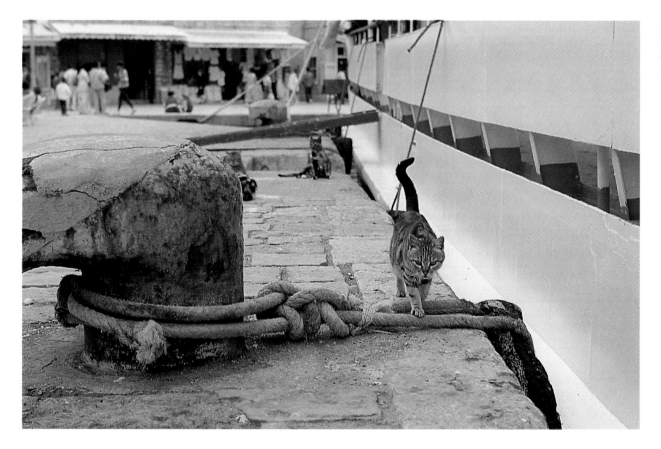

In Greece food for dockside cats is seasonal, arriving with each tourist boat in a summer glut.

Feral-cat caretaker feeds a neutered feral cat group in Florida, one of the first neuter-and-return projects in the United States.

Europe. In 1990 Werner Passanini, with David MacDonald of Oxford University, surveyed the effectiveness of neutering groups for the UFAW and concluded that it is the most effective way of managing feral cats.

As the neutering of colonies became more common in London, it brought down overall numbers. Whereas when I began to observe the Fitzroy Square colony, other cats occasionally attempted to enter the group, as years went by this became less frequent as other cat groups in the area were also neutered. As a control system, neutering is able to manage broad areas.

Despite this successful long track record in Britain, the technique became the center of a heated debate in the United States in 1993. During the early 1990s more than 400,000 cats a year were being destroyed in California's cat shelters, and welfare workers were looking for a way to reduce this. The National Audubon Society saw feral cats as a threat to wild birds and co-sponsored the AB 302 Feline Fix Bill, together with some cat welfare organizations, in an attempt to have it introduced in the California state legislature. The bill proposed to make feral cat carers the legal owners of the cats and insisted on the neutering of all

the carer's group within 30 days, with fines for noncompliance. The spectre of elderly cat feeders being "thrown in the slammer" became an alarming possibility. The situation was not just one of "cat people vs. bird people" but also "cat people vs. cat people."

More than 40 state and national animal groups formed Californians Against AB 302 to have the bill withdrawn. They declared:

"A feral cat care program aimed at spaying/neutering, vaccinating and feeding represents the grass roots animal control needed to get the problem of cat overpopulation under control. We will no more support a bill that criminalizes this work, threatens to hasten the impoundment and killing of cats, or threatens to fine those who do most work to stem the causes and symptoms of California's overpopulation of cats, than we will one that outright targets feral cats for impoundment."

The National Audubon Society's California legislative director was quoted in the press to the effect that his position on AB 302 was one of opposition to "any program which purports to trap, spay or neuter or return cats to the wild."

The lack of understanding of the effectiveness of the neuter-and-return technique mirrored that of Britain 20 years earlier, and the approach of the co-sponsors of the proposed bill was as if the system were new and untried. Yet in the United States, Alley Cat Allies (one of the signatories of the anti-AB 302) had been following the British experience and implementing the neuter-and-return method. They were not alone, for they surveyed 1,000 people working with feral cats across North America; 80 percent replied, and of these, 91 percent were using the neuter-and-return method.

To find out the experiences of the method outside the United States and to find a consensus among the cat welfare charities, in 1994 the Doris Day Foundation brought together a meeting of key organizations in Washington, D.C., and invited Jenny Remfry and me to address it. It was alarming to find that some charity organizers thought it better to put animals down to "save" them

from suffering that they *might* experience at some time. Some assumed that cats living a feral existence *must* be leading a terrible life, regardless of evidence to the contrary.

In a huge cat-owning society, opinions are bound to vary, but discussing differences is leading to a better understanding not only of the neuter-and-return method but also of the feral-living cat. While cats are no longer made divinities or demons, attitudes toward cats around the world are in a state of flux, and to some in America today the cat is a demon hunter.

Feral cats are great survivors and always manage to find secure shelter. Pipes are quite commonly used for this purpose.

Breeds and genetics

A champion British Blue is the epitome of the full-jowled male British Shorthair show cat.

```
              non-
      agouti  agouti
      Tabby   Tabby
       AA      aa

first
generation  Aa   Aa   Aa   Aa
all Tabbies

second     AA    Aa    Aa    aa
generation Tabby Tabby Tabby black
```

Mendel's 3:1 ratio from the mating of agouti and nonagouti cats (such as tabby and black cats).

UNDERSTANDABLE CAT GENETICS

In reality cat genetics are not simple, but in outline they follow a straightforward pattern — even if it is full of exceptions.

When Harrison Weir brought human manipulation of cat breeding into proper existence by inventing cat shows in the 19th century, he argued: "Why should not the cat that sits in front of us before the fire be an object of interest, and be selected for its colour, markings and form?" At the time there was no understanding of the mechanism of genetics, and his rules for breeding were the soundest advice available:

"In the first place, the fancier must thoroughly make up his mind as to the variety of form, colour, association of colours or markings by which he wishes to produce, if possible, perfection; and having done so, he must provide himself with such stock as, on being mated, are likely to bring such progeny as will enable him in due time to attain the end he has in view. He has to build up a family with certain points and qualities before he can actually embark in the real process of accurately matching and crossing so as to produce the results...he is hoping to gain eventually."

It was only at the beginning of this century that biologists stumbled on the obscurely published work of Gregor Mendel, who discovered the principles of heredity in the 1860s. Mendel's important breakthrough was to identify that characteristics are inherited by means of units that we now call genes, and he also discovered the working ratios in which these are passed on in successive generations.

We know now that genes are sections of chromosomes, made of DNA. Each chromosome is a chain of genes, and every body cell of the cat has 19 pairs. The special type of cell division for the sex cells makes each one have only 19 chromosomes. During the division that takes place to form individual sex cells, parts of one half of the divided chromosome may swap with parts of the other, which randomizes the genetic components. When adult sex cells fuse together on fertilization, they re-form a full complement of 38 chromosomes.

Each new kitten inherits a gene for

each characteristic from both of its parents. Early in the history of domestication, all coat colors and patterns were the same — mackerel tabby — so the coat genes were identical. The replication of the DNA during cell division for the sex cells produces an identical copy. However, mistakes can occur and be copied. This is a mutation. The original gene and its flawed image are termed alleles. Although an incredibly rare event, it is nonetheless the origin of the range of coat colors, types of coat, and other genetically changed characteristics in domestic cats today.

Most mutations are harmful and do not survive — but some do. The earliest known coat mutation was the appearance of the black cat. This is also seen in 13 species of wild cat and is called melanism.

Early cat breeders like Harrison Weir knew that if you crossed two apparently identical tabby cats, a black kitten or another solid color kitten could be among the litter of tabby kits. Usually one coat color is dominant over another, which is recessive. Tabby is dominant over black. To achieve consistent genetic results, Weir advocated that a "pure" family of tabbies would always breed true, and similarly a line of black cats would as well. If one of these tabbies and one of these black cats were mated, their offspring would all be genetically dominant tabby, but if two cats from this next generation were mated, there would be both tabby and black kittens, Mendel's ratio of 3:1.

The situation in the cat is complicated, because the tabby does not really disappear. Genetically all domestic cats remain tabbies, despite the evidence of your own eyes. Even in a solid-colored cat you can still see the bands of the tabby markings in a particular light. The tabby coat is an alternate pattern of solid color and flecking (called agouti, see pp. 23–24). An individual hair of a tabby is banded with yellow, which gives the agouti section, and in the solid color part of the coat this hair banding is absent and is called nonagouti. Consequently, the black and tabby cross is, genetically, really one of agouti and nonagouti.

When the alleles are the same in a pair, the cat is called homozygous for that characteristic; when it is mixed, it is termed heterozygous.

Some colors occur as a result of additional genes modifying others. Black is turned to chocolate by a further recessive gene. Black has an additional gene to be a full, dense color, but an allele of that will turn black to gray (called blue). This "dilution" gene changes the distribution of pigment in the hairs, so some incident light is reflected. Brown is diluted by the gene to lilac in the same way.

These types of straightforward results statistically occur readily in breeding with most of the

A three-year-old female Somali with its natural shaggy coat has the appearance of a historic breed, yet it has been developed over the last 30 years.

other coat colors that have historically mutated subsequent to black.

The Exceptional Ginger Gene

Some inheritance works by a more idiosyncratic manner, and that of the ginger or red color does in particular. It is usually assumed that genes are inherited randomly, but some genes are on the same chromosome and are inherited together, linked. One pair of the chromosomes dictate a cat's sex — females have a matched pair of chromosomes designated as XX, while males have an X and a Y. The rest of the chromosomes occur in matched pairs, but the Y is smaller than the X. While every ovum has an X chromosome, a sperm can have either an X or a Y. Consequently, any mutant allele, such as that for orange, carried on a sex chromosome, will be "sex-linked."

The Y chromosome does not have a site for an orange gene, so a male can only transmit the gene on the X chromosome and can only be orange (O) or non-orange (o). In contrast, a female, with two sites, can be orange (OO), tortoiseshell (Oo), or non-orange (oo).

There is nothing straightforward about the ginger gene, so although in a tortoiseshell female with Oo there are two alleles, there is an attempt to compensate for the male having only one. One of these alleles in each of the multiplying number of skin cells in the early embryo is ignored. This happens randomly, so a mosaic of orange and non-orange skin cells develops. The tortoiseshell queen develops this way, but if she also carries the gene for piebald spotting, and so has white as well, then the tortoiseshell pattern becomes more distinct; it is called calico in the United States.

On infinitely rare instances a cat has two X chromosomes and a Y chromosome, but these "males" are usually sterile. Some variations can be caused genetically by modifying groups of polygenes. Rufus polygenes enhance the degree of richness of color.

Incomplete Dominance

While most genetics work on the all-or-nothing basis of dominance or recessiveness, the notable exception is "incomplete dominance," in which both genes function but neither is dominant. The prime examples are the pointed cats of Southeast Asia. When a Seal-point Siamese is crossed with a traditional Burmese, a midway color appears of a less full color form of Burmese, but with coloring to the points. This is the Thai Copper and the West's Tonkinese.

THE BREEDS

The simplest view of "What is a breed?" is what is recognized as a breed by a registering body. Consequently, a breed in Britain may be different from what is considered a breed in the United States. However, from the biological perspective, the criteria for some modern breeds are trivial. In contrast, historic breeds have formed as a result of geographic and therefore genetic separation, so although their

A female tricolored Japanese Bobtail, orange, black and white, like the one below, is called the *mi-ke* cat. These cats were often depicted in 19th-century Japanese woodcuts.

development was aided by humanity, natural selection has largely been involved. These ancient types of cat are the most authentic of breeds and were formed long before the advent of the modern day cat fancy.

SHORTHAIRS

The British Shorthair should really be the robust moggie whose story was related in the preceding chapters, but during World War II, breeding was drastically reduced. Then, when pedigree numbers were low in Britain, they were bred for no good reason to foreign body shorthairs and then mated to Persians to correct the build. The result was a different cat. It is an attractive animal, but it does not represent its historic lineage. Its nose is inherited from the Persian.

The same happened in America, but the CFA called the new cat the Exotic Shorthair while retaining the name American Shorthair for what purports to be the all-American mog. Yet in the early days of the American cat fancy, British cats were mated with American cats.

The loss of the basic mog from British showing would have saddened Harrison Weir, who said: "A high-class, short-haired cat is one of the most perfect animals ever created."

The European Shorthair had the same traditional build, yet there could be distinctions in breed lines. The blue cats illustrate the differences between history and reality. Tradition informs us that Carthusian monks bred a distinct blue cat called the Chartreux. However, to keep the Chartreux in existence, cats

A colorful calico cat, tortoiseshell and white, makes an impression in Monet's garden at Giverny, France.

were mated with British Blues and Persians. The British Shorthair has a round head with broad muzzle, and ears set to the sides of the head. The Chartreux has a head that is broad at the top, tapering to a noticeably narrow muzzle, with ears set high on the head.

Fortunately, in the early 1980s in Scandinavia a group of breeders began the reinstitution of the selected mog as a show cat again, which led to the recognition of this European Shorthair

Top: This traditional-build brown tabby Persian is a homesteader's cat in Australia.

Above: The true Van cat is to be found in Van, Eastern Anatolia, Turkey. For the people of Van the features that make their cat special are the odd-colored eyes and a snow-white silky coat. The orange-marked cats recognized in the West do occur in Van but are not highly regarded.

by the Fédération Internationale Féline (FIFe). House cats have been shown in the novice class for European Shorthair at Cat Association of Britain shows, as the association is a member of FIFe.

LONGHAIRS

My earliest recollection of a cat goes back to my childhood days and to my grandparents' lovely old brown tabby Persian. It spent much of its time

comfortably asleep in the afternoon sun on the wooden lid of a massive water barrel at the back of their house. It was a fine cat of a type popular 40 years ago, with a fine, straight, unmessed-about nose and an old-style coat that did not need brushing.

Frances Simpson, the influential show judge, writing in 1903, shared some of my childhood sentiments:

"I cannot explain it, but certain it is that of all the feline race the warmest corner of my heart has always been kept for the brown tabbies [Persians]. There is something so comfortable and homely about these dear brownies — they seem to have more intelligent and expressive countenances than any other cats, and I am firmly of the opinion that no Persian cats are so healthy and strong as brown tabbies."

Angoras

Weir recalled that around 1850 most people referred to longhair cats as "French cats, as they were mostly imported from Paris and more particularly the white, which were the fashion." These were the Angoras that had been the pampered pets of the Ottoman Empire and had traveled to France to become the darlings of the 17th-century French court. In Britain in 1889, Weir was still able to distinguish between the Angora, the Persian, and the Russian, and these are distinctions that we can draw again today between the Angora, Persians, and Northern Longhairs, including the Russian.

However, by 1903 Frances Simpson could find "hardly any difference between Angoras and Persians," and the distinctions were so fine "that I must be pardoned if I ignore the class of cat commonly called Angora, which seems gradually to have disappeared from our midst." This happened as a result of indiscriminate breeding between all longhairs, regardless of origin. Fortunately, attention to historic and geographic integrity of breeds has again become recognized as important.

From Istanbul to Tehran, longhair cats can be found with a slim, warm-climate build. The genetic mutation selection for these longhairs has been favored by conditions that can inflict severe winters yet scorching summers. The Anatolian Angoras and Vans have an elegant long-faced appearance. The reappearance of the true Angora in the show world since the 1950s and 1960s has once again begun an appreciation in Europe and America of these most charming of cats.

Modern Persians

Persians of the form and build of my childhood companion shared something of their ancestors' build. However, breeding developed in Britain and Europe to foreshorten the animal's nose to what its devotees view as a more appealing face. To its detractors the flattened face gives a more pugnacious appearance. The adherents of the modern Persian longhairs are not concerned by the criticism that by imposing a flatter "baby" face and a fuller coat that needs daily brushing, they are perpetuating a dependent toy, but they believe that for the sake of appearance the extra grooming is a

requirement they are happy to meet.

In temperament, most Persians are usually docile and gentle. Their appearance has led to their long domination of the show bench.

Silver Tabbies, Smokes, and Chinchillas — An Inhibitor Sequence

The longhaired cat exists in an array of types, but some stunning coats began to be bred at the end of the last century. The Smoke Persian was granted its own class in 1893, and the Chinchilla followed in 1894. These emerged from breeding silver tabbies and form a series around an inhibitor gene.

In the silver tabby, the yellow banding is suppressed by the gene more than the dark lines, so the coat is black tabby on white. The Chinchilla has the most remarkable of marked coats, for it is as if the mist from the ghost of a tabby has kissed the tips of the hairs. Its delicate shading is caused by the inhibitor gene suppressing color in the hair except at the point where the hair first grows. The difference between the silver tabby and the Chinchilla is just one of degree effected by polygenes.

NORTH AMERICAN PEDIGREE REGISTRATION ORGANIZATIONS

ACA	American Cat Association
ACC	American Cat Council
ACFA	American Cat Fanciers' Association
CFA	Cat Fanciers' Association
CCFF	Crown Cat Fanciers' Federation
CFF	Cat Fanciers' Federation
NCFA	National Cat Fanciers' Association
TICA	The International Cat Association
UCF	United Cat Federation
CCA	Canadian Cat Association

The American Cat Association is the oldest American registry; the Cat Fanciers' Association is the largest American registry.

An 18-month-old female Blue Point Himalayan has the coat and build of the modern Persian.

51

The newer type Balinese sits alongside the older type (lying down).

The smoke is caused in the same way as the Chinchilla, but as it contains the nonagouti gene, its tipping is more noticeable and even.

In Cameo Longhairs, orange is swapped for black.

Colorpoint Longhairs — When East Meets West

One of the largest groups of current show-bench cats are the Colorpoint Longhairs, called Himalayan Persian in the United States. These cats are a blend of East and West, for they inherit points of color from the Siamese in the body of a modern Persian. While breeding research toward such a cat began early this century, in both Britain and America it was developed some 40 years ago.

To keep the predominantly Persian appearance, breeders usually cross Colorpoint Longhairs with Persians rather than with other Colorpoint Longhairs. The resultant solid-color Longhairs are then crossed with a Colorpoint Longhair because the colorpoint gene is recessive, and their litter yields both Colorpoint Longhairs and solid-color Longhairs. The result has been the Persian reinforcement that led to the cat being a coat-color class of Persian rather than a 50-50 blend and a separate breed.

OTHER LONGHAIRS

The Balinese

The Balinese is a longhaired mutation of the Siamese. It has the body of the Siamese and flowing silky hair. It retains the outgoing, talkative nature of the Siamese but shares with the Angora a nearly tangle-free coat and still retains an elegant long nose. In recent years the conformation of the Balinese has pursued a more svelte form.

The Birman

The Birman shares the Siamese points and the

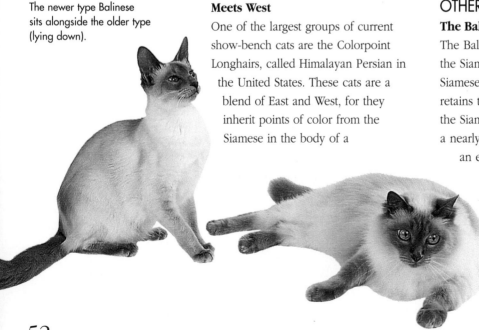

build of the earlier-bodied Siamese breed type. Its white feet are the distinctive feature. There is a belief that the white feet derive from the cats from Lao-Tsun Temple in Burma. A folklore story suggests a supernatural origin for the first cat's white feet from contact with its dying companion, the priest Mun-Ha.

The Somali

As the Balinese is to the Siamese, so the Somali is to the Abyssinian. It is one of the most striking of cats, and because of its ticked coat, has "the soul of the wild." The Somali probably originated as a mutation, but it has been argued that the recessive longhair gene stems from early outcrossings to Longhairs.

NORTHERN LONGHAIRS

For those who prefer the older, rugged style of Longhair, the growing interest in the various Northern Longhairs has been met with enthusiasm. The massive presence of the Maine Coon cat from New England has a growing following in the Old World. In the United States they are most popular.

The similar Norwegian Forest cat is equally robust and has a similar homestead background.

ORIENTAL AND FOREIGN SHORTHAIRS

Previously in Britain, under GCCF ruling, the term *foreign* was applied to all Shorthairs except the British type, and *oriental* was used for patterned coats. Since 1991 Siamese-derived cats are dubbed oriental and all others are

classified as foreign. The term *foreign* is still generic for conformation and consequently is applied to Rex cats, despite the geographical inaccuracy.

The cats of East Asia are distinct from those of European ancestry. Among street cats in East Asia, one of the most noticeable genetic modifications is the kinky tail, which occurs in two out of three cats. Its abundance suggests that cats were introduced to the tip of the Malay Peninsula by Arab and Indian seafarers centuries before any European

Top: The magnificent Maine Coon lived as a semiferal farm cat in New England, where its full coat protected it from the harsh snow-bound winters of Maine.

Above: The Norwegian Forest cat shares the Maine Coon's weatherproof warm coat. The Danish Racekatte, the Swedish Rugkatt, and the Russian Longhair are the geographic equivalents of the Norwegian Skaukatt.

exploration. Only a few cats arrived initially, and a malformation in the tail of a cat in this early population became widespread. It does not carry the dangers of the Manx gene.

The extreme form of kinky tail, which reduces the tail to a rabbitlike bobtail, is the basis of the Japanese Bobtail, which has a long history. The slender build of the original cats from the Mediterranean ancestry has been retained in the warm climate of Southeast Asia.

In Thailand centuries ago, the *Cat Book Poems* were written down under royal instruction; these document the Siamese, Korat, and Copper and reveal the antiquity of these breeds.

The Siamese

The Siamese was the consort of the monarchs of Siam and was presented to certain visiting dignitaries in the 19th century. Its remarkable appearance with dark points at the first cat show in 1871 caused a sensation and was a major factor in the show's success. Initially Siamese in the West were imported only in the dark sealpoint, but gradually the hidden inheritance of recessive and color-dilution genes gave the blue, chocolate, and lilac classic Siamese colors.

Among the temple cats of Thailand there are other colorpoints that have arisen by natural crossing. Breeders in the West have extended the Siamese inheritance into Longhairs, making it the main coat determinant (after the underlying tabby) in the show-cat world.

The Burmese

The Burmese was once believed to have been a breeder's invention in the West, as it appeared when a U.S. Navy psychiatrist took home a brown cat from Rangoon in 1930 called Wong Mau; it showed some point darkening.

It was crossed with a Siamese, and then the kittens were crossed back to Wong Mau. In the litter, along with Siamese offspring, were also brown cats and a rich dark chocolate cat that was designated Burmese.

Brown cats were termed Thong Daeng, or Coppers, in the *Cat Book Poems*. I found both Coppers and full Burmese feral in Thailand. Breeders in the West of the Tonkinese — the remade Copper of the East — were delighted to learn that the breed had a history and could be found today.

Burmese are currently a "smart" cat for the young owner who would not be seen dead with a fluffy modern Persian, but who feels that he or she needs to be "upmarket" of a moggie.

Opposite top: American Professor Edward Rose and his wife, Malee, are shown at their breeding cattery in Chiang Mai, Thailand. He is holding two young Burmese, the progeny of the robust Copper stud tom called Woot held by Malee. This is part of a program to broaden the Burmese genetic base in the West with genes from the original area.

Opposite below: In the illustrations in a Thai manuscript, *Cat Book Poems*, the upper cat is a depiction of the Siamese, or Vichien Mat.

The Siamese, the "Royal Cat of Siam," in its authentic original build, in Thailand.

Top: The Korat is considered a good luck cat in Thailand. Its late acceptance in the West has protected it from the build changes inflicted on the Siamese and Burmese. The Korat's eye color changes from gold to green at around 2 years old.

Above: The Russian Blue's distinctiveness was threatened when before World War I Russians were judged to the same standard as British Blues.

Opposite top: A Persian in the United States is recognizable as a Peke-faced breed.

Opposite below: A young female chocolate Oriental Spotted Tabby displays its Siamese origins.

Unfortunately, fashion has moved the Burmese toward a slighter build in Britain, while the original form has been retained in the United States.

The Korat *vs.* the Russian Blue

The blue cat from the Korat province of East Thailand is one of the true gems of the cat world. Originally the farmers' cat of Thailand, it was termed Si-Sawat in the *Cat Book Poems*, which noted that its "eyes shine like dewdrops." It is a gentle but lively cat and popular with breeders today in Thailand.

Although shown in Britain at the end of the last century, the Korat was ignored because the Russian Blue was already established. The Russian Blue's arrival was attributed to sailors bringing it from Archangel.

Even when the Korat became

established 30 years ago in America and was then reintroduced to Britain, there was again resistance because of similarities to the Russian Blue. Confusion was not aided by a post-World War II outcrossing of Russian Blues with Siamese blue points to change them to a more foreign type. However, during the 1960s Russian Blue breeders did a 180° turn in an effort to regain the original conformation. The Korat eventually won acceptance.

The Oriental Shorthair Selfs

In the early 1950s, at the time that the brown Burmese were being introduced into Britain from the United States, breeders in Britain bred a solid brown cat from the chocolate point Siamese. This was followed by a foreign-built white, a lilac, then a black. At the time it was not realized that Siamese-bodied solid-color cats already existed in Thailand.

Spots and Stripes

Slim, foreign-build tabbies exist in abundance in Southeast Asia, and gloriously spotted ones in India and at the birthplace of the species in Egypt and around the Mediterranean. Spotted cats from Egypt gave rise to the Egyptian Mau breed developed in the United States in the 1950s.

Despite this, breeders in Britain pursued a re-creation of the early Egyptian cats, starting with a Siamese-form tabby. This gave rise to the Oriental Spotted Tabby, which was briefly also called the Mau in Britain. Each of the Siamese-derived cats exhibits the behavior patterns of the Siamese, but being of the thinner contemporary form, is more active than its traditionally shaped relatives.

THE CHANGING CAT

The formation of new breeds has come about this century as a result of crossing and mutation selection. Unlike in cats, mutation selection in dog breeding has retained a wide range of shapes and sizes. Unfortunately, the transition from work to showing led to numerous inheritable problems. Many large dog breeds have a tendency to hip displasia. Present-day bulldogs are a travesty of their predecessors, as their foreshortened faces make breathing difficult and their disproportionately large heads cause significant problems in giving birth.

In the cat show world as yet, the genetic problems are not so widespread. However, there is a clear need to take stock now before such concerns are common among cats.

Almost inevitably, breeding and judging to a written standard take a breed away from its forebears. The two most notable changes that have affected the largest number of breed cats are to the nose of the Persian (Longhair) and the build of the Siamese. Fortunately for Persians (Longhairs) in Britain, a halt was called to the trend, but in the United States it continued and led to the recognition of the Peke-faced Persian. However, in Britain the accentuated form termed the "ultra" has caused concern.

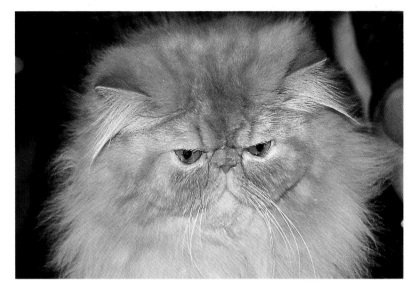

The flat-faced Persians have a kitten-shaped face as an adult cat; yet this shape can cause problems. At a cat show in the United States years ago, I remember in particular one cat that was the center of its owner's attention and affection. It was therefore very sad to watch as she repeatedly dabbed away the tears that continually fell down its cheeks before she took it for judging. It was a good-natured animal, but to walk the two steps from the center to the front of its cage to greet me left it wheezing.

The promotion of a hairless mutation as a breed termed the Sphynx has caused serious controversy.

Selection for thinner Siamese cats has led to a change of head profile and skull shape.

Breathing difficulties and faulty teeth are common in these cats. Even among apparently "good type" cats at shows, there is a likelihood of running eyes, as the draining ducts are kinked and compressed. On some white show Persians, this can leave a reddish staining that is treated daily with an antibiotic.

I am firmly in favor of the stand taken by the Governing Council of the Cat Fancy, which is against the recognition of this breed in Britain. I argue that to choose to inflict distress, to breed to perpetuate disadvantage, is wrong and should be regarded as unacceptable as other causes taken up by animal welfare campaigners today. For me it is an animal rights issue.

In North America the most popular shorthair show cat, the Siamese, has disastrously collapsed. While 20 years ago the benches of any major show would have been teeming with Siamese, by 1990 they had all but disappeared. When the Siamese first arrived in the West, they were seen as exotic, but they were firm, robust animals. Yet

recent fashion dictated that they should become more "foreign" than the real thing. The trend toward thinner animals resulted in frailer cats that were hard to breed, vulnerable to illness, and increasingly uneconomic as they became less popular to own.

Unfortunately, awarding schedule points can push toward unhealthy extremes, and judges need to be aware of not exaggerating trends to the disadvantage of the breed. Part of my *Cats* series that looked at modern breeding trends elicited a particularly strong reaction among many viewers worried by mutation selection for weirdness rather than for good-looking cats. Although dogs have undergone drastic changes in appearance as a result of breeding, in cats this is unprecedented. Domestic cats have looked after their own breeding for 3,500 years, and function was paramount for survival. Yet in a matter of a few decades people are now causing serious problems.

Novelty or Alarming Trends

I prefer a cat to look like a cat. Breeding to enhance and not disadvantage the animal is a fair guideline. Unfortunately, reasoning is not always straightforward. The longhair kittens appearing in Siamese litters before 1950 were put down as freaks, yet the Balinese line that developed from later identical kittens is delightful. Since 1950 other conditions previously considered genetic abnormalities have been adopted as a basis for a breed.

In the 1930s Rex cats were viewed as

freaks. Yet 40 years later they had gained acceptance. The next step, a move away from the normal coat, caused dismay to many people. In 1966 the naked Sphynx cat was born in Canada and was developed into a line in North America. There is something distasteful about a judge looking for "nice wrinkling of the skin" at a show.

Ears, too, have been changed. In Scotland in 1961, a cat was found with flattened ears. The line that developed was disallowed registration by the GCCF in Britain but was acknowledged by the CFA. Thus, North America became the center for Scottish Fold breeding. Breeding must be to nonfold cats, for the homozygote has spina bifida and gross thickening of the cartilage in the feet and around the joints that prevents walking. In California in 1981 a cat with ears bent backward instead of forward became the American Curl.

How far will people go in the pursuit of the bizarre regardless of the animal's welfare? Potentially there is a "four-eared" breed, as cats have been born with an extra pair of ears. However, the head was oddly shaped and the animal

was inactive, which may have been the result of damaged brain function. What was once indefensible may now be snapped up, for the hype used to popularize the Ragdoll in the United States was based upon its lethargic inactivity — it was "ideal for apartments."

Cats with short legs were reported in the 1930s and 1940s. This is now proposed as a breed in the U.S. as the mutation has reappeared and been given the name Munchkin. Because of its stumpy legs, it cannot jump like a normal cat. This has startled many people, yet the American geneticist Solveig Pflueger says it is caused by the same gene as in the Corgi. However, given the problems in reduced-leg dogs, that is not reassuring.

Cats were born earlier this century with stunted front legs but normal-length back ones, which dramatically affected how they walked. In sitting up, the unfortunate animals were described as looking like small kangaroos. What a

Ear movements and positions are a key part of cat-to-cat communication. The American Curl (left) and the Scottish Fold (above) are mutations with permanently distorted ears.

The American Ragdoll, seen here with its original California breeder, goes limp on being handled — hence the name. Although this behavior is the characteristic on which the breed was based, breeders in Britain are now seeking to achieve the appearance without the limpness, which has been criticized.

This stumpy-legged mutation has been called the Munchkin after the little people in *The Wizard of Oz*. The choice of "cute" names for disadvantaged mutations unfortunately seems to make their being considered as a breed more acceptable.

grotesque selling point that could become for a new "breed." Will the genetically inherited split-foot and hare-lip become the basis for new breeds? At what point should a line be drawn?

It could be argued that as cat breeding is of minority interest, why worry? Yet now that responsible pet ownership has led to around 80 percent of house cats being neutered, there is an increasing influx of breed cats into the house cat population. While in the hands of responsible breeders, problems should be restricted, but as the circle widens,

controls will be harder to implement, and Pandora's box will be opened.

Harrison Weir left his beloved Crystal Palace cat shows when he found some owners more interested in prizes than in the welfare of the cat. Judging from his comments when discussing breeding, some of today's changes to the cat would horrify him:

"There are rules which ought to produce certain properties that may be desired, either by foolish fashion, or the production of absolute beauty of form, markings in colours, or other brilliant effects, and which the true fanciers endeavour to obtain. It is to the latter I shall address, rather than to the reproduction of the curious, the inelegant, or the deformed, such as an undesirable number of toes, which are impediments to utility."

Our judgment is sometimes clouded by considerations that are not in the best interests of the cat. The Manx is the classic case: it is a historically regarded breed, yet a genetic nightmare.

The Changing Cat — Conclusion

Registering bodies worldwide should disallow any physically disadvantaged type of cat proposed for breed status in the future. Those who love the cat should not damage it or promote its damage. It is within the hands of us all to ensure that cats remain the supremely beautiful, healthy, independent animals that they have always been, and that we do not ruin what we love, leaving as our inheritance a genetically damaged and physically crippled animal.

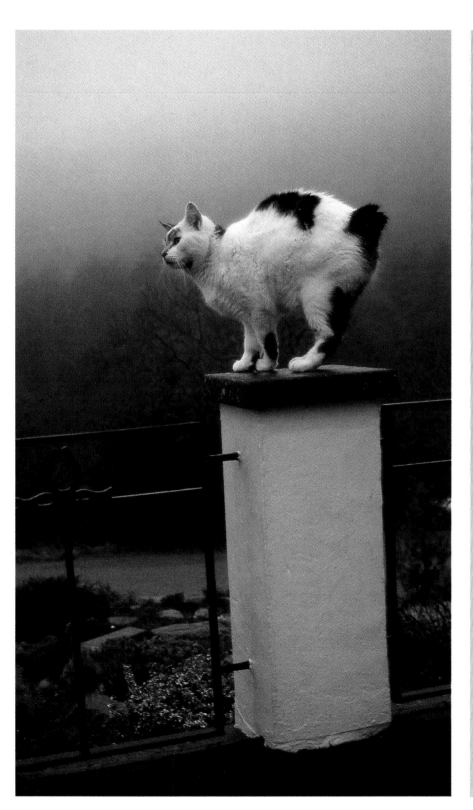

THE HISTORIC CASE — THE MANX

The earliest record of the Manx cat from the Isle of Man is of those owned by the painter Turner in 1810. It was commonly believed they had developed from cats that had had their tails cut off and had bred tailless kittens.

As a historic breed, the Manx has an associated folklore and is part of the national Manx identity. Having spent time on the island with the indigenous cats, I can vouch for their charm and distinctiveness. But if this mutation occurred today, it would be considered too dangerous to breed.

The Manx gene is dominant, but homozygotes die before birth. Even among heterozygotes, malformation causes a high rate of stillbirths, and consequently it is a lethal gene. The surviving cats range from having some tail to the "Rumpy" exhibition form without tail vertebrae. In this state some degree of spina bifida is common, and the pelvis and spine can be fused, restricting the cat's gait.

America has become the center for breeding. Some years ago the Manx parliament, worried that the cat would disappear from the island, set up a government cattery. After ups and downs, it was bought out by a private couple who closed it down because they were concerned about the welfare of the cats. Once again breeding on the island has returned to the cats themselves, which is perhaps the best outcome.

Structure
for function

The contrast between the Chinchilla's coat and the black rim of its eyes gives it a particularly dramatic appearance.

MAKING SENSE

Cats have specialized sense organs that enable them to exploit their nocturnal, semi-arboreal lifestyle. Nonetheless, many owners attribute additional abilities to their pets. A Cats Protection League survey found that 56 percent of owners believed that their cats had psychic abilities.

Reflect on Cats' Eyes

The cat as hunter has forward-facing eyes. Herbivorous prey species have near all-around vision by having eyes on the sides of their heads.

We share a similar eye structure with the cat, but they have specialized adaptations for night life. Cats can see at a light level one-sixth of the amount that we require. Relatively, they have the largest eyes of all domestic animals. Consequently, they have proportionally larger pupils and can let in more light at night. The cat takes in 50 percent more light than we do. To maximize light intake, cats' eyes have a large lens, and the cornea is noticeably rounded, giving them a "glassy-eyed" profile.

This feline nocturnal advantage would be a huge daytime disadvantage without a compensating arrangement in the iris. In most big cats the pupil shuts down in a circular way, but more tightly than ours. The pupil of the domestic cat and other small cats narrows to a slit, for it needs extremely fine control to avoid dazzle.

The key feature for which cats' eyes are known is their reflective quality, which lent "divine powers" in Ancient Egypt, demonic ones in medieval Europe, and emulation in road markers. The reflection is caused by a crystal mirror, the tapetum lucidum. As there are few photons of light in dim conditions, any that miss detection in the retina on arrival are reflected back from the mirror behind the eye to give the retina another chance. The tapetum does not function until kittens reach 12 to

14 weeks, when the need to hunt at night arises.

Cats' eyes have another feature that we do not share — the nictitating membrane, or third eyelid. It is white and often comes as a shock to owners when they see only a white void instead of the eyeball. It is perfectly natural and will sometimes cover the pupil when the cat is dozing, allowing light in but obscuring all detail. As soon as a shadow crosses the eye, the membrane flicks aside and the cat is alert. If something enters the eye, the membrane can become inflamed, and it can drift across the eye when your cat is feeling ill. Unexpectedly, as cats do not have the

protective antibacterial enzyme lysozyme in their tears, they blink infrequently, at times only once in five minutes.

Hearing

For the night-hunting cat, finely attuned hearing is vital. When your cat hears prey, it is instantly alert, with pricked-up ears. Even while it is sitting on your lap, its ear cones, or pinna, turn about like radar sweeps. We can hardly move our ears at all, but the cat's pinna have more than 20 working muscles that allow the ears to turn sufficiently well to pick up sounds from behind the head. The cat's ability to detect sounds with precision is reduced if it makes

COLOR VISION

Cats can see color, but only at a fraction of our ability. This apparent loss has been traded for a great gain in nocturnal vision. At low light levels we find the landscape drained of color saturation. In both our eyes and cats' eyes, there are light receptors in the retina – cones discriminate color, and rods are more sensitive at low light levels. Three different types of cones work at different wavelengths to interpret the color spectrum, similar to the working of a color TV system. Rods give the equivalent of a black-and-white television picture. With a ratio of 25 rods to 1 cone, in contrast to our 4 to 1, cats' sensitivity in low light levels is massively increased. Behavioral and physiological studies over the years have shown that the little color that cats can see is primarily green, with a minute amount of blue.

Even though this cat is lying down, it is alert of eye and ear. At the lower outer edge of the ear, the pocket termed the bursa allows flexibility in the ear's movements.

The cat's nose is sensitive to temperature as well as scent.

dog's prey does not make much high-frequency sound, unlike the small mammals and birds hunted by the cat.

Physiological responses have been found at 100kHz, but the realistic upper area of normal hearing above which sensitivity is low is around 35–65kHz. In practical terms, cats have been trained to respond to tones up to 60kHz. Rodents' squeaks are in the 20–50kHz range, which is mainly above the normal human responsive limit of 15–20kHz, but exactly in the region of good sensitivity of the cat. Although physiological responses for dogs have been found at 60kHz, their realistic upper area for normal hearing is found to be in the 15–35kHz range.

On the underside of the cat's skull toward the rear corners are two large bulbous areas called the auditory bulla, housing the inner ears. Their formation in Aeluroidea is different from that in most mammals. The bulla create an air space internal to the tympanic membrane, and seem to allow resonances to particular frequencies and give a greater sensitivity to those frequencies. The cat's disproportionate sensitivity to rustling sounds made by small prey may be due to resonances forming within the cat's ear to those sound frequencies.

Sensing Scents

Inside the cat's nose, separated by a nasal septum, is a labyrinth of bony, platelike projections, the conchae, which almost fill the space. These are covered by an olfactory mucosa providing a surface of around 3–6

directional swivels on the move, so most are made while the cat is frozen motionless. The same muscles allow the cat its great range of facial expressions, even to the extent of laying the ears flat.

One of the enigmas of the cat's ear is the bursa. Although this flattened pocket at the outer angle of the pinna seems to have no obvious function, it allows the ear to fold and move, and it may also dampen complex sounds received from behind the head and assist localization. Cats identify the source of a sound mainly by detecting a difference in the intensity of the sound between the ears. Cats detect sounds at different heights better than dogs are able to, which accords with the cat's semi-arboreal hunting.

It comes as a surprise to most people that the dog's ability to hear in the ultra-sonic is less than the cat's. However, the square inches — twice the human amount. In the mucosa are olfactory cells that detect the volatile substances that waft in. These cells are only at the top back of the cavity, to which air penetrates only on definite sniffing by the cat rather than just breathing.

Tasting Scent — "Flehmen"

Below the floor of the nasal cavity are curved cartilage tubes, the vomeronasal organ, or Jacobson's organ, which connects to small holes behind the upper incisor teeth. This organ enables the cat to "taste scent" by gaping and adopting a curious trancelike state when sniffing at cat urine or some other scent: the "Flehmen response." This German word has no ready counterpart in English; "grimacing," although the nearest equivalent, does not accurately convey the action.

The Jacobson's organ is only rudimentary in humans, so we cannot appreciate the information it could yield. However, in most animals it seems strongly linked with sexual behavior. The organ is connected to

A classic tabby gives a characteristic Flehmen response to a scent, its mouth held open.

65

The cat's spiny papillae are most pronounced in the middle of its tongue.

When seen magnified by a scanning electron microscope, the papillae themselves look like a mass of small tongues on the tongue.

the medial hypothalamus, which is involved in sexual activity, and the ventro-medial nucleus, which is involved with feeding control.

The Flehmen response of the cat family to the urine marks of other cats may be linked to sex hormones in the urine. The tiger's Flehmen response is dramatic, as it appears to look disgusted, although clearly it isn't. The domestic cat's Flehmen gaping action, despite its importance to the cat, usually goes unnoticed by owners. Both toms and queens make the response.

A Tongue of Taste

Whenever a cat licks your hand, you are in direct contact with one of the cat's most useful tools — its tongue — and it is a rough contact. The Aeluroidea have the most developed bumpy tongue of all mammals. The

upper surface of the tongue is covered with a series of backward-pointing spines, or papillae, which give it many uses, from combing the coat and rasping food to taking up more water to drink via the surface tension effects of the spines. The cat's tongue fulfills functions for which we use our hands. Consequently, the cat accepts stroking as the equivalent of being licked.

The cat does not have taste buds on the central spiny papillae, but on the more rounded papillae at the front, back, and sides of the tongue. The tastes interpreted by most mammals are sweet, sour, salty, and bitter, but cats alone show no particular response to sugars. The ultimate carnivore, the cat enjoys a meat diet, rich in protein and fats but virtually devoid of sweet tastes. Kittens do receive milk sugar, lactose, when suckling from their mother, but lactose levels that cause no problems to newborns can cause severe diarrhea in weaning kittens. Milk is a major cause of diarrhea in many cats.

A Touching Ability

The skin's specialized nerve endings pass on messages along the nerves on receiving contact pressure. These vary over the cat from 25 in a square centimeter of skin on parts of the head and feet, down to 7 in a square centimeter of the back, tail or ears.

The cat's nose, tongue, and paw pads are most sensitive.

The Cat's Whiskers

We realize how special they are when we say that something terrific is "the cat's whiskers." The cat's normal hairs, particularly the coat's longer guard hairs, are connected to touch detectors, so it is small wonder that after you stroke a cat, it combs the hair back into place with its tongue. The whiskers are enlarged hairs especially endowed with sensory receptors.

When a cat yawns, the muzzle whiskers sweep forward in an array.

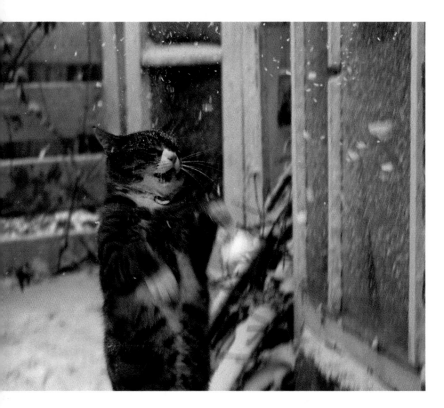

When snow first falls, some cats go wild with enjoyment as they play with the strange stuff, regardless of its being cold and wet.

Those around the mouth feed information about the width of openings, which is as vital for going through a fence hole in the urban jungle as in dense woodlands when prowling around after dark. The muzzle whiskers are part of a circular facial array of whiskers, with superciliary tufts above the eyes and genal tufts on either side of the face behind the main whiskers. In the dark we put out our hands to feel our way, while cats, because they are leading with their heads, use their whiskers.

Unlike other carnivores, cats have no tufts under the chin. The gain of extra power in the bite of a cat by the foreshortening of the face length has left no room for such a set of whiskers. The most unnoticed whiskers are on the underside of the foreleg, but these are vital for the arboreal cat to judge landings. They also help the stalking hunter and aid prey catching with its paws.

The cat's expressions are enhanced by its muzzle whiskers. During yawning, they sweep forward, while when the cat is being anxiously defensive, they are flat back against its face.

TEMPERATURE DETECTION AND CONTROL

Cats love warmth. The cat curled by the fire is taken as a sign of contentment, yet ironically, the curled-up cat is a cool cat trying to control heat loss. The true warm, contented cat by the fire lies out long to lose heat. My cats often sit closer to the kitchen range than I find comfortable, for while I can tolerate a temperature only up to 115°F (44°C), cats are happy to stay up to 125°F (52°C). The cat's nose and upper lip act as its key external thermometer.

Acclimatization experiments have shown that the cat can habituate over a wide range of temperatures. It has shown this ability by living feral, generation after generation, from the equator to the subantarctic. Cats have a thicker winter coat, and the transition to a thinner summer coat is dramatic in breeds like the Angora and Van.

The color points of the Siamese coat are temperature dependent; at lower temperatures more pigment is made. Because the points are cooler than the body, they are where the color develops.

Our cooling control is by the evaporation of sweat. Cats cannot have watery sweat all over their fur, as it would increase the evaporation surface, so their watery sweat glands are restricted to the bare skin surface of their feet, around their nipples, and lips.

The dog, as an animal of pursuit, cools its body temperature by excessive panting. In contrast, cats, which primarily work by stealth, try to avoid becoming overhot in the first place and strenuously avoid too much exercise for its own sake.

CAT CLAWS

An essential part of the felid makeup is the claws, which, like a fistful of switchblades, are protractable — not retractable, as is so often stated. At rest they are sheathed and have to be actively protruded. Consequently, unless the cat is old or its claws are very long, any clawing of your furniture is intended. All cats can protract their claws and share this ability with some other arboreal carnivores. Cats sheathe their claws to keep them from being blunted as they walk on the ground but keep these climbing spikes ready for use. This has given them the added advantage of available hunting and fighting weapons. In contrast, the dog has blunt claws because it walks on them all the time.

When cats catch prey, unlike dogs they first engage with their claws. The small cats that pursue small prey initially make contact with paws and claws extended. Only when the prey is subdued do they bring their head forward to bite.

THE SUPREME HUNTER'S DESIGN
Branching Out — The Tail and Other Parts

The cat's design and build is that of a woodland hunter. It moves effortlessly amid tree branches, aided by the

balancing movements of its tail.

The fastest cat, the cheetah, uses its tail as a gyroscope to turn at speed without falling over. Our cats use the same technique as they clamber about — if balance is threatened, the tail comes into play.

Lying out long is a clear sign of a warm cat. They lie back to expose their tummies and lose heat. Curled cats, in contrast, are cool rather than contented.

The cat's whiskers help it to judge close distances as it climbs, aided by its specialized protractable claws.

The Sense of Balance

In the inner ear, arising from the fluid-filled cochlea, are three semicircular canals. These canals are at a 90° angle to each other. When the cat makes any sudden movement, the fluid tends to stay put, and relative movement is detected by tiny hairs. This gives the cat its sense of balance.

We have a similar system, but unlike the tree-clambering cat, we do not have a self-righting reflex. Because cats can fall from trees, this rotating mechanism is a definite survival advantage. The cat's ability to rotate rapidly when falling is incredible and reveals a highly attuned gravitational detection, for it needs to know when to stop rotating. This information is partly provided by sight, but also by minute pieces of chalk in the semicircular canal system, which land on the hair cells from the fluid.

Time

The cat's sense of time is remarkably accurate: if you feed your cat at a set time, it will turn up virtually to the minute. However, if cats are put in continuous darkness, their internal biological clock begins to drift. Morning light seems important for resetting this biological clock.

ESP AND PSI

Many people want to believe that cats have extrasensory perception. It is strange that we want the cat, with its finely honed senses, to have yet more, but since it can "taste scent," why not? Many believe that cats have super-navigational abilities. Birds migrate in part by using magnetic detection. Bees navigate via the sun's position. So if the cat does have good navigational ability, it is less likely to be extrasensory perception and more likely to be perception via an extra sense. But do they have it?

I am frequently told of cats finding their way back to their old homes when their owners have moved. When I have investigated, it seems cats have found their way back to the old home over unfamiliar ground, at least over relatively short distances. There is no need to suspect magic, for if the cat's attachment to its home range is strong, then it may feel the need to return. As other animals can navigate via natural phenomena, so perhaps can the cat.

What is harder to believe are the rare claims made that cats that have been left behind have been able to navigate to their owner's new home. That does seem impossible unless people send out "vibes" like homing beacons. Yet one New York vet moved across the United States to California, and some months later a cat just like his old one turned up. He was skeptical until, he claims, he found the cat had an identical bone injury to his old cat. The term "psi-trailing" has been coined to cover such almost impossible journeys.

The arboreal cat has a ready ease while clambering high up among small branches. Its sure balance is greatly helped by its tail.

Sex – cats and their kittens

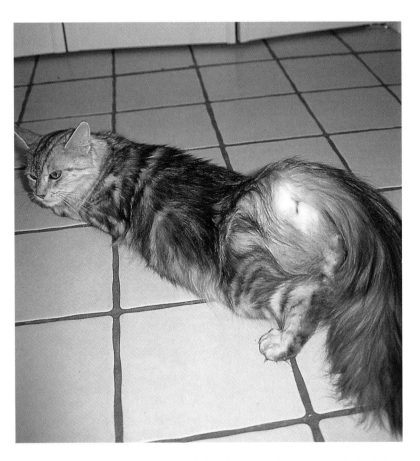

(Above) A Maine Coon queen in the lordosis position solicits the attention of a male and demonstrates her readiness to mate.

(Top right) A queen is rolling "in heat."

THE SEXUAL CAT

The cat has always been synonymous with sex. We still talk of a sexually demanding woman as "a cat in heat." The cat's dramatic sex life made it the perfect candidate to become the fertility goddess Bastet in ancient Egypt. According to Aristotle in 350 B.C., "the female cat is particularly lecherous, and wheedles the male on to sexual commerce." Aelian in A.D. 120 noted that "the male is extremely lustful, but the female cat is devoted to her kittens, and tries to avoid sexual intercourse with the male because the semen which he ejaculates is exceedingly hot like fire, and burns the female organ."

The witchcraft era held to the belief of "seed of fire" but interpreted the cat's apparent sexual excesses as wantonness and wickedness. The reality is no less dramatic. Female cats go through several cycles per year of sexual responsiveness. Breeders' cats that are housed or cats that live in warm climates will come into season earlier in the year than in the more northern climates. The timing seems to be controlled mainly by light levels. Cold weather and low light physiologically dampen the ardor of street cats. This is no accident, for post-weaning survival of kittens can depend on the mother's ability to catch sufficient prey to feed the young.

As she comes into season, the female's behavior changes, and she begins to call and advertise her state. Her sexual scent and sounds encourage interest from toms, but initially she will not accept their approach. Her estrus state lasts for up to four or five days, during which she rubs her head and chin on objects, rolls about, and crouches low with her rear raised, and rhythmically paws the ground.

When the queen's hindquarters are raised — the position termed lordosis — the male makes quiet, chirplike calls to her and can increase her responsiveness by licking her vulva.

The male often needs the reassurance that he has a right to be present, and to mate successfully some toms need time to establish "residence," in part by scent marking. A young, inexperienced male can be intimidated by an aggressive queen, such that his first successful mating can be delayed by months.

While the queen rubs her head on the ground, the male approaches indirectly, moving around her. He moves and normally grasps the loose skin at her neck. He then mounts, adopting a hugging grip with his forepaws around her body. Copulation at a breeder's may take only some 10 seconds, but in free-living cats can take $1\frac{1}{2}$–2 minutes.

Edward Topsell expressed the event in the 17th century in an unusually tolerant way for the time:

The manner of their copulation is this, the female lyeth downe and the male standeth, and their females are above

While mounting, the male secures a firm hold of the queen by grasping her by the scruff of her neck.

measure desirous of procreation, for which they provoke the male, and if he yeeld not to their lust they beate him and claw him, but it is only for love and not for lust.

The one-to-one relationship between male and female that occurs in the confines of a breeder's cattery is far from normal; when cats are free-ranging, the scents and calls of the queens cause a number of toms to gather. The friction caused as toms have to pass through each other's territories has long been noted. Bartholomeus Anglicus wrote in the mid-13th century:

In time of love is hard fighting for wives, and one scratcheth and rendeth the other grievously with biting and with claws. And he maketh a ruthful noise and ghastful, when one proffereth to fight with another.

A scanning electron micrograph of the male cat's penis shows the spines that trigger ovulation in the queen.

This is based on shrewd observations, for the caterwauling that many attribute to mating occurs earlier and is due to the threats that prelude fights. The nocturnal "cat-song" in suburban areas is just as likely to indicate straight-forward territorial disputes.

However, there is a scream that the queen emits that is at the heart of sex in cats. Unlike women and most other female mammals who release an egg as part of their regular sex hormone cycle, cats share with a few other carnivores the need for stimulation to induce the egg's release. Male cats have a small bone in their penis called a baculum, but the particularly unusual feature of the organ is that its flanks are covered with backward-pointing spines. These also occur in other carnivores that are induced ovulators. I found that on the cat there are between 130 and 190 spines, and the more sexually mature the male, the larger the spines. Neutering reduces the androgen levels, and so the castrated male's spines regress. The spines are the anatomical feature that caused our ancestors to talk of "seed of fire," for they cause the female to react violently and scream at the point of withdrawal. The barbs ensure that mating with the first tom triggers the release of the egg, which then travels down the fallopian tubes until it reaches the site where it can be fertilized, a journey that takes many hours and during which the female cat mates with numerous toms.

In many mammals mistiming of mating and ovulation is a major cause of infertility. In the cat the male's curious anatomy linked to the female's need for induced ovulation prevents this problem.

The cat's wild ancestors were spread out by their elaborate territorial system, and this way of mating bought time to allow toms from different areas to congregate and so prevented the double problem of missing ovulation and inbreeding within a group. This is the system our cats have inherited. Ovulation occurs around 24 hours after the first mating, and fertilization follows at between 24 and 36 hours after copulation.

Few studies have been made that look specifically at mating within large groups of free-living cats, but a recent one by Eugenia Natoli and Emanuele Dé Vito on the groups of feral cats living among ruins in the center of Rome has cast light on the secret sex life of the cat by following the queens that came in heat. During the course of a queen's estrus, she would be courted by 8 to 20 males, and although at any particular mating session there would be as many as 15 males around her, 5 was most common. Most females copulated with more than one male during their estrus period, some with up to 7 males.

An important feature of cat mating that emerged from this study is that significantly there were 2.5 times more mounts taking place without intromission than those with full mating. The average was 29 without intromission and 11 with intromission for a queen in 24 hours. For the average queen, that amounts to 39 sexual acts in

24 hours, or 1 every 38 minutes. Small wonder that the ancient Egyptians made the cat the female goddess of fertility.

I found in my study of East London house cats that some toms will make appeasing overtures to the early pro-estrus queen to try to move closer to her. She will allow his approach to a certain distance but then stop him. This different strategy, in contrast to charging directly in, has also been found in the Rome study. Although the Italian researchers found it did not seem to matter which strategy was used with regard to the outcome, from my London observations it seems that less assertive males may successfully pursue their end via this route and minimize the risk of fighting with dominant toms.

After mating, the female normally rolls onto the ground, and both male and female will separately wash.

When cats are in the controlled conditions of a breeder, or there happens to be only one male around with free-ranging cats, the male initially does all the running, while the female is not that eager. As time goes on, he becomes more tired, while her enthusiasm grows. When more males congregate, which is the more usual case in this situation, a more even balance is achieved.

The apparent nymphomania of the female cat is concomitant to the species' territorial patterns, which themselves emerged from the way of life imposed on this carnivore by its forest ancestry. Its behavior, design, and way of life mesh as a survival package. The multiple matings, in addition to ensuring

A traditional-build Siamese queen in Thailand lies with her newborn kittens. As they grow older, they will develop the color on their points.

fertility, give further advantages, as they can produce different sires to a single litter, increasing genetic diversity in a group. Cats that live with and around us in urban settings live at fantastically higher densities than they would if we were not on the scene. Consequently, more males can be present at a mating than could have occurred historically, so genetic diversity is being accelerated. This has been offset in recent years by the increase in neutering in the town house cat and feral populations.

THE BIRTH

If you have had your cat mated and she conceives, she will miss her next heat and then her nipples will redden and become more pronounced. At three to five weeks after mating, a vet should be able to check for pregnancy by very gently feeling her abdomen.

As the embryos turn into developing kittens, they become a nutritional

A mother cat purrs and rhythmically paws as her two-day-old kittens suckle.

drain on the mother, and she will gradually eat more from around the fifth week of pregnancy. From six weeks onward, her larger size will be noticeable to the eye. As her size increases, she will spend more time resting and will often lie on her side, as she will do later when suckling, for this spreads the weight of the developing kittens.

Overall, her pregnancy will last around nine weeks. As her term approaches, she will begin to look for a kittening spot and probably will accept the offer of a cardboard box cut down on one side and with newspaper bedding. This should be put in a warm, quiet, dark corner. However, she may prefer her own choice.

Virtually all cats manage to give birth with no problems and without the need for human intervention. Certainly advise your vet of your cat's condition, but a

vet will need to be involved only if the cat becomes distressed. In a feral group or multicat household, other females may assist. Queens often purr throughout the process of giving birth.

The queen will lie down in a semi-prone position, with her upper rear leg partly raised, and a vaginal discharge will occur. This can go on for some time, but once contractions start and she begins to strain, she should give birth to a kitten in its sac after 15 to 30 minutes. The mother's rough tongue will lick away the sac and wash the kitten. Her licking will also stimulate the kitten to take its first breath of air. She will cut through the umbilical cord herself, eat the afterbirth, and clean up around the kittens. The time between the births can vary considerably, and although the average number of kittens is four, this can also vary.

It was suggested earlier this century

that since house cats can have up to three litters per year, while the forest wildcat, *Felis silvestris*, typically has only one, this constituted a clear difference between the domestic cat and its main ancestor. However, I found that by analyzing the trapping data on the feral cats and kittens of Stichting De Zwerfkat in Amsterdam, one litter per year seems to be normal for feral cats, with the peak being in April and May. It seems that it is not domestication but domestic living that allows the house cat to have late litters, and that living wild, the domestic cat is more like the wildcat in normally having only one litter a year.

TIMETABLE OF KITTEN DEVELOPMENT

It is impossible not to fall in love with a little kitten. When people go to a cattery and see some kittens, they often cannot resist taking one home. The reason for this is that, besides looking small, fluffy, and cute, they have a flatter face with proportionately bigger eyes than their parents. This appeals to us, for they are the features of our own babies.

The First Two Weeks

There is a definite timetable for kitten development. When kittens are born, it is the beginning of a big adventure in which at first they are totally dependent on their mother's support. In the first 1 to 2 days, the kittens receive the vital colostrum from their mother, which gives them their initial immunity, after which they thrive on their mother's normal rich milk. She feeds them completely for the first few weeks.

A litter of 10-day-old kittens at the "blob" stage huddle together for warmth. One is making a defensive hiss outward.

The new kittens have to find food, despite the fact that their eyes are shut until day 5 to 10, and that they have minimal hearing until day 5. They navigate their way to the teat by their sense of smell and also by homing in on warmth. The mother helps by lying on her side, exposing her teats, and nuzzling the kittens in the right direction. Their sense of touch has been with them from before birth in the womb and is now used fully.

While puppies have little loyalty to any teat, kittens do develop a preference. This is an advantage for the mother, as even young kittens have sharp claws that could damage her teats in a squabble. Even at a very young age, the paws open and the claws protrude as the kitten "kneads" while suckling their mother.

When kittens begin to feed, they engage in long, 8-hour suckling sessions. From very early on, they will squeak to the mother to let her know that they want food or that they have

Top: At 2½ weeks the kitten's ears are still small, and its shaky legs cannot lift its tummy clear of the ground.

Above: The kitten at 4 weeks old, has longer ears, and legs strong enough to stand at full height.

out of the nest huddle, they work their way back in, pushing their heads into its midst. Their small legs are not strong or long enough to lift their tummies off the ground, so they drag themselves in a wobbly way back to the warmth and security of the others or to find a teat.

I find that during the first 2 weeks, before their eyes bring them focused information, the kittens, with their eyes shut or open, will open their mouths wide and give a defensive hiss when the strange scent of an intruder reaches them.

Two Weeks Old

When the kittens' eyes first open, they are very cloudy and bring in little information. During their third week, although their walking movements are still shaky and they stay in a huddle, the kittens will sit up on their haunches properly for the first time and *look* at things. If you are around, some of them will look *at* you, and they certainly recognize their mother. The automatic defensive hiss disappears. Some eye fluid cloudiness will remain for another few weeks. The ears are still small in proportion to the round face at these early kitten stages.

Three Weeks Old

When kittens reach 3 weeks old, they begin to explore the world. They discover how to walk, placing their paws down in a fairly shaky way. As they begin to move around, the litter mates enter properly into the activity of play with each other.

strayed away from her into the cold.

During their first 2 weeks kittens seem like cute little unsteady blobs, for their heads are quite round and their ears quite small. They have a strong desire to stay in a heap huddled together in the nest when the mother steps out. Their noses are sensitive thermometers, and if they are

Five Weeks Old

At 4½ to 5 weeks, kittens are more robust. If you sit with them, they are able to clamber up your clothes, albeit in a slow and lumbering way. They begin to mountaineer but may need some help. Their vision is now good. The cloudiness in their eyes has disappeared completely, and the eyes have become sparkling clear. The kittens had some hearing on day one, but now it is very good. Hearing will continue to improve until they are 12 weeks old. By 5 weeks old, they are gaining that much more information on their world, and they make more sense of life.

At this age the excreta of feral kittens would normally begin to change from that of just a diet of milk to that which includes the occasional mouse. In cats that live with people, the change is to cat food.

While the mother cat has been content to lick away the mess from her kittens' rear ends, its new constituent changes her mind. For survival, the mother prevents the appearance of detectable mess around her nest while the young are too small to be very mobile. As the mother's cleaning behavior changes, the kitten no longer needs her stimulation to eliminate.

The play of 5-week-old kittens is much more firm in movement. They arch and thump down more determinedly on litter mates. They jump up and down and bat their fellow kittens quite heavily.

Seven Weeks Old

At 7 weeks kittens are usually weaned and are eating solids; suckling ceases. They are often taken away to their new homes at this stage. The kittens are now more self-possessed and they are much more coordinated. In their play they turn to pursuit games as if they are after prey, and they now play more with objects. Their improved sensory input lets them have better body

Top: A Maine Coon kitten has bright eyes and large ears, is just weaned, and is dashing about.

Above: Two black-and-white 5-week-old kittens still suckle. To help stimulate the milk flow, they open and close their paws, pushing at the teat.

At 5 weeks old kittens begin to clamber — but not too well.

Eight to 14 Weeks Old

Once a kitten reaches 10 to 11 weeks old, its motor coordination is fully developed, so potentially it has all the flexibility and movement control of an adult cat.

From 8 weeks onward, kittens are beginning to react like adult cats toward a threatening situation, so play begins to change again. At around 9 weeks old, play between kittens becomes more earnestly aggressive, and squabbles can become spats. These are still rehearsals for the adult world, so there are lulls in the rushing around that let the "protagonists" get their breath back.

Until kittens are around 12 to 14 weeks old, the level of playful interaction between kittens remains high, and a lot of it is as much about object pursuit, running around objects, and generally investigating as it is about scrapping. By 14 weeks, the aggression has seriously weakened the youthful bonds, and the litter dissolves as adulthood opens before the now independent juvenile cats.

Sensitive Periods: Learning for Adulthood

Sensitive periods used to be called critical periods, implying that there was a once-and-for-all learning period. Now, however, biologists recognize that cats can also learn later in life, if not so well. Nonetheless, it is better if the kitten can learn at the right stage; otherwise, it can take much longer.

One such window of learning is around 4 weeks, when the mother

control, so their play noticeably changes. The mother's behavior also changes as weaning progresses. She no longer lies back exposing all her teats but begins to roll over slightly to cover up her nipples if the kittens are still demanding. Their reflex to right themselves if they fall off something has now developed, just in time to be useful, since life has now become more of a scramble.

begins to bring home prey for the kittens. Up until this stage, all they have encountered is their mother's milk, so it must seem strange to the kittens suddenly to see a dead mouse. But during this sensitive period kittens are very trusting — they believe whatever mother gives them is good for them. The kittens need to have this acceptance and trust of whatever the mother brings in; otherwise, when she brings back live prey, they might become frightened.

The mother starts by bringing home dead prey; after a while she graduates them to subdued injured prey and eventually to lively prey by the time they are weaned. She trains them by acting like a competing kitten. Their interest is stimulated and they learn about prey by handling it. Her apparent competition then increases.

Handling Kittens

Sigmund Freud would be pleased that the cat world is beginning to catch up with his pioneering work on evaluating the adult from what happened in childhood. Even today in most catteries, whether those of breeders or of cat shelters, there is little time set aside for handling young kittens. Much of the effort put in by breeders to get the appearance of the cat right can be negated by paying no attention to kittenhood behavioral development. What usually happens is that people service the enclosure of mother and kittens by providing food, changing the litter, and keeping it clean. Particularly during the "blob" stage of

up to 3 weeks, actually entering and handling the kittens can seem like invading their sanctuary.

In reality, that is exactly what is happening, for among cats living feral the mother will make strenuous efforts to avoid having her kittens put at risk

Below: A 6-week-old kitten adopts the classic position demonstrating fear/aggression: fluffed-up full tail and arched back, side facing the other kittens.

Bottom: Seven-week-old littermates take part in the rough and tumble of boisterous play.

Seven-week-old littermates compete over a mouse.

by anything, and she will move them whenever she feels it is necessary. However, despite this strong protective urge, it has long been known that mother cats will bring up other animals in their litter alongside their kittens. Harrison Weir noted in his observations of 1889: "They [cats] will rear other animals such as rats, rabbits, squirrels, puppies, hedgehogs; and, when motherly inclined, will take to almost anything, even to a young pigeon."

If prey species are brought into the nest area by the mother in the normal sequence of dead to an increasingly live state, from when the kittens are 5 weeks old in anticipation of weaning at 7 weeks onward, the kittens will recognize them as prey. However, before that time in the biological timetable, intruders should not be in the nest, and if they are planted by devious means, the kittens will accept them, as clearly the mother has allowed them into their "safe haven." The kittens behave toward such cohabiting animals as fellow littermates, and as was

shown by researchers more than 30 years ago, they will continue to behave differently toward that species for the rest of their lives.

Our intruding into the kittens' nest and handling them should be seen in that perspective. When we handle kittens and they habituate to people, it is not because of some magic influence of people; rather, we are taking advantage of the kittens' development, which will help to put them more at ease with people in later life. Eileen Karsh in Philadelphia in the late 1980s began to investigate the differences that earlier handling could make. Compared to kittens with no handling, she found that post-weaning handling made little difference to their friendliness when they became adults. In contrast, earlier handling from between 2 and 3 weeks until weaning at 7 weeks turned kittens into much more sociable cats with humans later in life. This would seem to be the cat's sensitive window for socializing with people. Although kittens should not be removed from their mother until weaned, they should be handled by people earlier than is customary. It is better that such gentle handling should be in the nest area to avoid causing separation anxiety and later behavioral problems.

If you go to a cattery and bring a kitten home once it is weaned, you will naturally lavish love and attention on it. Unfortunately, this will probably be the first time for your kitten to experience such handling, and it will be too late to condition the kitten fully to people. Well before you go to any cattery, call and inquire whether, as policy, someone spends some time each day gently handling the kittens in their nest area. It is certainly not a good idea to remove a kitten from its mother before weaning, for that in itself will cause behavioral trauma and it can become fearful and aggressive with people and other cats. But time spent by people with pre-weaned kittens in breeding catteries and shelters is not wasted time.

Habituated kittens will fit even more comfortably into human households for the rest of their lives, having discovered that we are not monsters.

SEXING KITTENS

When you are looking for a kitten for your household, it is fairly important to *know* its sex, and not just to be told what it is. It is not uncommon for Tom to change to Tabitha as you discover after a while that the advice was carelessly given.

The basic rule is that on the rear end of a female kitten the apertures of the vulva and anus are close together. In the male the apertures, this time of the penis and the anus, are farther apart to allow for the position of the testes.

If you have any doubts about what *close* and *farther apart* mean, look at a few of the other kittens in the litter, and you will soon recognize the relative distances.

Six-week-old Abyssinian kittens — at a very appealing age — nestle together.

The territorial cat

Secure in its territory, a house cat sleeps in one of its preferred sunning spots — and by its presence and way of "nesting" declares its ownership.

Uniquely among domestic animals, the cat defines its own use of land, while with cattle, horses, dogs, or gerbils, we tether, fence, or cage them and impose their area of use. However, we have no need to contain cats, for they know where the edges and limits are on their own ranges. The cat determines the edge of its range as a consequence of a number of factors.

In everyday English we often use the word *territory* to cover anything connecting an animal with its land, yet technically to the behaviorist, a cat's territory is that area of land it will defend against other cats. The area that

it uses on a day-to-day basis is its home range, and although it is often quite similar, invariably it is larger than the territory. In reality, neither are fixed entities, and the area utilized varies at different times of year and also depends on other changeable factors, such as a new cat next door.

It is not just cats that play this game, for we recognize our own territorial boundaries by the hedge or fence between our garden and the neighbor's. Yet we range farther as we go about our daily lives. The cat does not consider a fence by itself a territorial limit. A cat living on the other side of the fence will change its significance.

In rural areas a cat's range can be large, as there are few competing cats about. In a suburban landscape cats live more closely packed together. In essence, however, there is little difference in the pattern of land use, just in its size.

To the ecologist the key factor about the home range is that its size has to be sufficiently large to provide the food needs of the animal. So the richness of the pickings in the landscape dictates how far a wild or feral cat has to range to survive. Consequently, the carrying capacity of rural hillsides for feral and farm cats is much lower than that of urban and suburban areas, where

densities of house cats are high because of the superabundance of food. As a result, a well-fed suburban cat does not need a large range, and the presence of neighboring cats ensures it is confined. In that sense, territorial considerations set the limits on the size of a cat's home range beyond that of the minimum area for food requirements. The boundary between two female cats can be recognized by the way they sit on their own side and stare at each other.

Suburban queens can hold parallel ranges in a series of adjacent gardens. Toms are different. An intact tom may range over an area up to 10 times the size of the range of a local queen.

A cat wakes up and stretches before setting off on the rounds of its territory. It shares the core area of its range with other cats around the house.

Between sleeping times, life is an earnest business of watching for territorial intruders.

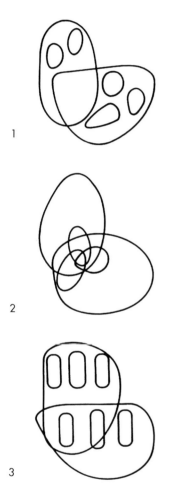

1

2

3

The patterns of home ranges of cats: the larger loops represent male ranges and the smaller loops those of females.

1 The normal wild cat range pattern; also the feral cat range pattern where food is dispersed and scarce.
2 The clumped ranges of feral cats around a locally abundant food source.
3 The ranges of house cats.

CAT RANGES

The cat's semi-social life works on the balance of food and range, and one dictates the other. If a cat has a ready source of food, it does not need to travel so far for food and consequently does not need a large range. In the Highlands of Scotland, where there is little food to scavenge and most has to be hunted, a feral cat needs a huge range. At the other extreme, the density of cats is high in town centers, even for feral cats that can scavenge food from garbage cans, bins, and plastic bags and also receive handouts. The highest density of cats is achieved by house cats; we virtually pour food down their throats, so they do not need much space.

The densest area in the world for cats is suburbia, with small backyard gardens. The remarkable feature is that from range studies of tigers and European forest cats as well as domestic cats living feral, the overall land-use pattern for the cat family is consistent. Yet why is the male's range up to 10 times larger than that of the female? It does not need to eat 10 times more food than the female, for although it is larger, it is not *that* much larger. The reason is social. The female is the basic unit, and her range is the minimum size that can support a cat. We often assume the male cat is idle when it comes to rearing young. The female tiger and tabby first suckle, then bring back food for their kittens without any apparent involvement from the male. However, the male does expend a massive amount of energy patrolling and

A territorial dispute between neighboring neutered house cats takes place at their boundary fence. The female aggressor has fluffed up her tail and back, while the male is standing sideways with arched back to appear larger. Like most disputes, it did not become a fight, and all moves were in slow motion. Its significance is that it shows to each cat the current willingness to retest and redefend limits that are fluid.

protecting the huge range within which a number of females may rear their young.

If food is spread out and thin on the ground, female feral cats, like wild cats, do not overlap their ranges. Yet if there is a rich local source of food, they will readily clump their ranges around it. The toms will also clump their ranges but wander farther and still give a protective buffer zone to their group's queens from other cats or cat groups. This is what happens around a group of garbage cans or where cats are fed in an urban square by a feeder.

Our relationship with our own house cats is also governed by this ratio and pattern of land use. If you live in a house with a queen, she will identify with your use of your garden. Other queens identify with their owners as individual groups in a series of parallel ranges along a stretch of gardens. If you own a tom, it will hold a larger range than the local queens. It will recognize their areas and then range relative to them up to 10 times the area if he is intact and up to about 7 times if neutered.

The tom's range will naturally overlap a number of queen's ranges. But whereas historically or in a feral state, a tom could expect that the queens he overlaps territorially would relate to him, in the suburban landscape of house cats, each of the queens will identify with her owners as a group member and perceive the tom as an outsider — modern suburban life can be hard on the male of the species.

Paths and Snoozing Spots

Whatever the size of your garden and your house, there are places your cat just does not visit, for it has particular paths. It will also have preferred snoozing spots. Cats take great care with their temperature control (see pp. 68–69) and move between favorite warmer and cooler places within their range.

When basking in the sun, cats manufacture vitamin D from the action of the sun on 7-dehydrocholesterol on their coats, which they ingest when they groom. The cat confined indoors does not usually have this advantage but will sit in the sun as it filters through the window glass. However, it still alternates between warm spots, such as by a radiator or under a table lamp, and cool spots, such as behind the sofa. For cats, particularly on cooler days, one of the advantages of sitting on people's laps is that they can absorb the warmth.

As winter approaches, cats progressively spend more time in the warm indoors and as a result put less effort into maintaining the size of their exterior territory.

Snoozing indoors or outside, the cat is ever-watchful for territorial incursions.

YOUR PLACE IN YOUR CAT'S GROUP

In many ways I behave toward my cats as if they were human — and I'm not alone in that. Similarly, to my cats I am some sort of cat. We are all a bit confused on the overlap between people and pets.

When you look at how your cat forms its range, it becomes clear that it relates to you as if you were a cat. Our cats do not look to us to build defensive barricades, so while they won't regard a fence as a limit just because it's there, they do look to see where and how we use space. If you never go into your garden, your cat may well have no particular attachment to it. If instead you love to sit in the garden, take afternoon tea, and bask in the sun, you will have a companion alongside. Nothing will bring a cat to sit beside you so quickly as doing a spot of weeding — the curious cat will come to see what you are doing. You are sharing an identity of land usage. While a fence may not necessarily demonstrate ownership to the cat, it recognizes your presence as declaring ownership of an area and gains confidence of its right to be there because you are there.

Scent Marking

Cats, being small animals, do not have the advantage, which we take for granted, of being able to see over things into the distance. Our gardens and both rural and urban environments can seem as much a jungle to them as the landscapes of their ancestors. In consequence, the ability to leave scent marks around their range helps them to read the landscape to see if it is unassailably theirs or if other cats are about. Scent marks are one of the ways that other cats know where your cat has territorial presence, even when it is not around. As a cat moves around its range, it has some indication of time from scent marking: not only does scent age, but other cats may have overlaid or intruded on the scent since the cat was last there.

A cat leaves scent not just around its range but on other group members as well, and that includes us. When cats rub against us and when we stroke them, reciprocal scent messages are left that are nonthreatening and behaviorally supportive within a cat group. We may be unable to interpret such scents, but the cat's life involves checking scent directly and by taste while washing all the time. The Jacobson's organ over the roof of its mouth (see p. 65) is able to aid such investigation. You may have noticed that your cat will investigate your shoes and trousers very closely, with its nose almost glued to them, after you return from somewhere that has other cats. Your cat may suddenly stop and go into the held gape of a Flehmen response as it allows the scents to be brought into the organ and interpreted. This happens in both sexes of the cat. Our return into the house with a cardboard box of shopping similarly elicits a full inquiry. If cats are interpreting such smells as originating within their range or just out of it, we must surely cause them some consternation.

There are scent glands on a cat's head and on the top of its tail near the body, so when a cat rubs against us, it is leaving a scent. However, it also has huge sebaceous scent glands along its lips and chin. (If a cat develops acne

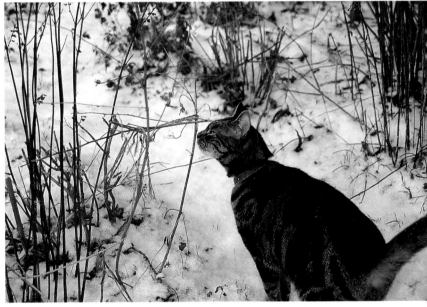

on its chin or "stud tail," the glands are blocked or overproducing wax.) When cats walk around their range and leave information about their presence, they use these glands. The action by which they frequently and carefully rub against a small twig or dried stem of grass sticking out in their path is called chinning. This movement as the cat brushes against objects can be almost

Top: A neutered queen stops for "chinning" on the ground in response to finding an interesting scent there.

Above: A neutered female house cat checks out a "scent stick" that another cat has marked by brushing against it.

imperceptible, but it is enough to leave a residual scent — a message. If you have not noticed these extremely significant signposts, squat down to cat height and they will become obvious — obvious enough that other cats recognize them and go straight to them to check them out.

If you watch your cat as it goes out the door or through the cat flap into the larger world, it does not usually charge out but moves carefully, checking as it goes. As a cat passes through a gap in a fence or through its cat flap, it will deliberately leave a deposit of grease from the coat, which other cats will then be able to check out by sniffing.

The linkage of group identity between ourselves and our cats can sometimes be "one removed" — "one removed" meaning unclean transferred behavior. When a shy cat wants to rub against us but is too nervous to come close, it will carry out the same action by rubbing against an adjacent object.

Broadcasting a Message by Spray

The pungent scent spray of a tom broadcasts its presence widely. As the position and shape of particular twigs elicit the chinning response, so certain shapes and positions, such as a low wall, elicit spraying from an intact tom. Because intact males are often intent on asserting their territories, they will especially mark by spraying key strategic places that may be disputed. Consequently, you may find your cat flap sprayed by a local tom as it detects the scent of your cat from the aromatic coat oils accumulated on the flap. If you have a timid cat, it will find such a situation quite stressful, particularly if it has previously been attacked by an intruder. Hubcaps on cars are frequently used and checked by cats because of their shape and size and because they are at a comfortable height for the tom to spray against.

Although an intact tom's spray is strong enough to be read at a distance, at times other cats will go up to it and give a Flehmen response. While spraying by an intact tom is directed against a vertical object such as a wall, neuters and queens are more likely to spray against a horizontal object.

However, when asserting a right to be in a territorially contested spot, a neuter may well spray vertically like an intact tom, but its spray will lack the characteristic smell.

Scents are particularly significant to other cats, for not only do they declare the right of presence, they also convey information on sexual condition. Because the spray can be a bit strong for us, it is one of the main reasons that owners have toms neutered.

Opposite top: Territorial marking of branches on a tree in the cat's area: the cat rubs with the side of its mouth, leaving a scent from skin glands and saliva.

Opposite below: A Maine Coon working farm cat in Maine checks a rubbing point to see if another cat has marked it since it last marked itself.

Below: Spraying is universal throughout the cat world. Here a cheetah sprays in exactly the same way as a domestic tomcat would.

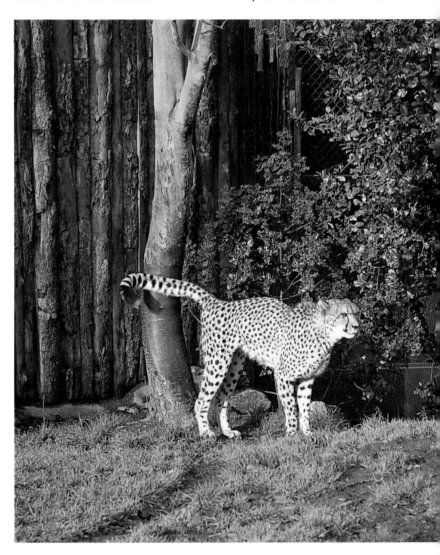

Territorial Clawing

When a cat rears up against a tree with outstretched paws and drags its claws through the bark, a number of events are going on, one of which is scent marking. Certainly the cat is sharpening its claws, for by dragging them through the bark, moon-shaped shards of keratin splinter on each side, bringing the claw to a point. Cats are fussy about the type of tree they will use, preferring something like a young fruit tree or established pine tree that has bark soft enough for the claws to sink in and be pulled through. Claws are blunted as cats walk on our concrete-clad landscape, so they need to resharpen them periodically.

Although cats enjoy the action of stretching, and clawing on a vertical object, they will do the same on fallen timber. The action is the same characteristic move that the cat makes when it wakes from a snooze, takes a couple of steps forward, and while keeping its hindquarters raised, stretches out its front paws and makes a long curve of its body. The only difference is that the clawing is added.

However, this action is multi-purpose, which is appropriate for an animal that does not like to waste effort. Cats have very few sweat glands on their body; being small furry animals, they would lose too much heat through evaporation. They do have watery ecrine sweat glands on their feet that keep the skin supple, so they retain touch sensitivity in their pads. As nocturnal hunters, they need information on the nature of the surface they are walking on. They are as cautious of walking on thick mud or gravel as they are of walking on thorns. When cats claw a tree, they leave faint scent messages from their sweaty feet, which would be ignored by other cats but for the visual claw marks that draw their attention, and they sniff these.

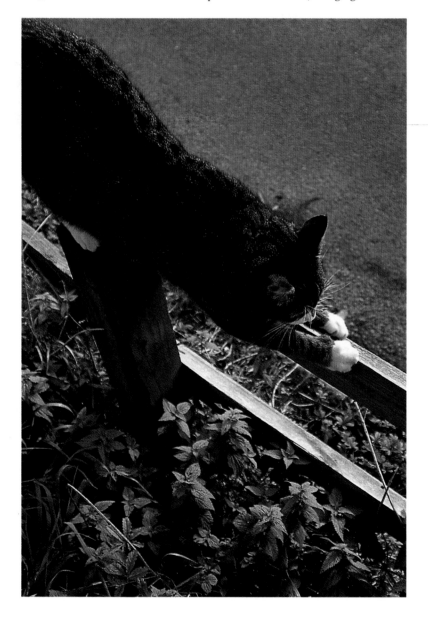

Although clawing is commonly carried out against a vertical tree, it is often done on fallen timber or, as here, on a horizontal fence rail.

Dropping the Scent

Many animals use their droppings for territorial scent marking, and the cat is no exception. It is unique among domestic animals in burying its feces, but not always, and in that lies a flexible scent-marking role. If you watch your cat as it covers up its droppings, you will see that it carefully checks the scent to ensure they are smothered. Covering does not destroy the scent but extends it by preventing it from drying out quickly; at the same time, however, the scent becomes more discreet.

Dominant toms, though, often leave droppings exposed in areas of dispute, in the manner of a fox, to assert their authority. It need not be just a dominant tom but one sufficiently confident to claim a presence. As an example, my neuter tom Leroy developed an infected abscess following an attack by a dominant tom. On his return from the vet, he was kept in for a week to recover, but during the day I took him for a walk on a lead through a field that his rival had claimed. For the first few days Leroy deposited his dung very visibly on top of flat grass knolls until he considered these were sufficient to claim a right, and he subsequently returned to burying his droppings. During this same period he sprayed vertically against bushes, which he normally would not do, and he chinned a lot. He also growled at his rival on sight, and my presence ensured that he maintained his confidence during these meetings.

However, when after a gap of a week I took him along the same route, for the first few days again he left his droppings prominently sited and made no attempt to cover them, in contrast to his normal behavior within his own range.

Cats usually prefer to leave their droppings semi-peripherally to their confident range, but they are restricted by available sites. Lawns and concrete are not enticing, and gardens with weeds and rain-packed soil present few opportunities, but the next-door neighbor's fine tilth is ideal. His vegetable plot is excellent for both ease of digging and position. If you loathe cats and find your garden is a communal toilet, your best defense is to have a cat of your own and your garden will be dug up less.

When cats dig, they take their weight on their back legs and, alternating their front paws, dig toward themselves, digging deeper as they go. In average garden soil, some 22 paw scoops are usual. When the cat is using its dug latrine, it adopts a characteristic position with its tail up, at up to 50° from the horizontal. If, as a behaviorist, you need to be able to tell whether a cat is defecating or urinating, you do not have to be too indelicate, since heaving sides are the clue to the former action. The cat will then sniff and cover and repeat until the job is done.

Cats also have scent sacs on either side of their anus that are lined with secretory cells whose production is linked to hormone levels. These may add scent information to feces. They are also a secret scent communicator, for when we stroke a cat or when cats greet each other, their tails whip up, exposing the urinogenital area and the scents.

A queen adopts a characteristic pose after digging a latrine in a neighbor's gravel path.

The hunter supreme

A mole lying on its back defends itself from a cat that has taken it back into its home. The cat's whiskers have been brought down toward the mole and will give the cat instant information on contact with the prey.

HOW THE CAT HUNTS

The cat employs different hunting techniques for different types of prey. For a bird in the garden it tries a variant of the dash-and-freeze party game. It keeps its body slung low so that its shoulder blades stand high, like those of a cheetah. The bird has a range of advantages. It has a huge field of view, reaching a full circle in some species. It also has a facility most frustrating to the cat — flight. If that were not bad enough, most give shrieking alarm calls that put other birds on their guard.

Cats are most successful at catching garden songbirds in the early summer, when there is an abundance of ill-equipped fledglings. The young birds' parents are at their busiest and may take risks.

Young rabbits, in the first month after they come aboveground at 2 months old, are a favored prey. These are stalked, and the inexperienced youngsters are easily surprised.

For small mammals, particularly short-tailed field voles, which live on the surface of the ground under the cover of grass stems, the attention of cats is suddenly caught by their sound. Having homed in on a vole's position with its ear cones and sitting stock still, the cat then rears up and pounces down with its front paws together in exactly the same manner as a fox. If successful, it gathers up its prey straightaway. If not, it thumps the place in the grass a few more times using smaller moves. Out of the grass the cat is unlikely to rear up, but attacks directly with its paws.

Small mammals, such as mice and voles, will seek cover for protection, but if forced out into the open or taken by the cat into a more open patch and released, they will run along the side of walls, rocks, or fallen trunks. The cat will attempt to bat the animal with its paw to stop its escape.

Why Play with Prey?

Even the keenest cat owner is uneasy about a cat playing with its prey. The cat is superbly armed to deliver a death blow, so why on earth doesn't it just get on with it? If owners were cat-sized, they would soon see why. Cats go in paws first with their heads well back. Only when they are totally sure they

The arch hunter Leroy pursues a yellow-necked mouse.

are not going to be bitten do they bring their mouth into position. But with their short faces they share with us the inability to see what is going on around the mouth. The neck bite that is a feature of the cat kill requires a very intimate positioning at the back of the victim's neck. If the prey moves, or even worse, bites back, the cat is in trouble. Consequently, it matters to the cat that the prey is not only fully subdued but stunned so that it can safely make the kill.

Even a shrew can be a daunting opponent, for it will turn onto its back and threaten the cat with its teeth. When a large prey such as an adult rat is pursued (which will be undertaken only by a very confident cat that has learned the necessary technique), the retaliatory threat is much more alarming. A rearing adult rat is a formidable opponent to a cat.

What seems like playing with live prey is an earnest strategy played out between two skilled players. While the raining of paws onto the head of a rat to suppress it is a gladiatorial battle, to most onlookers the same technique used against a small mouse seems hardly fair because of the size difference. Yet it is a fairer match than it appears at first, for a good percentage of prey escapes.

A cat takes its prey back into our homes as its feral cousins take theirs back into the core area of their range. It seems a crazy move, for we are highly likely to say "Get that thing out of here," while among a feral group the overlapping area is where other group members are most likely to be

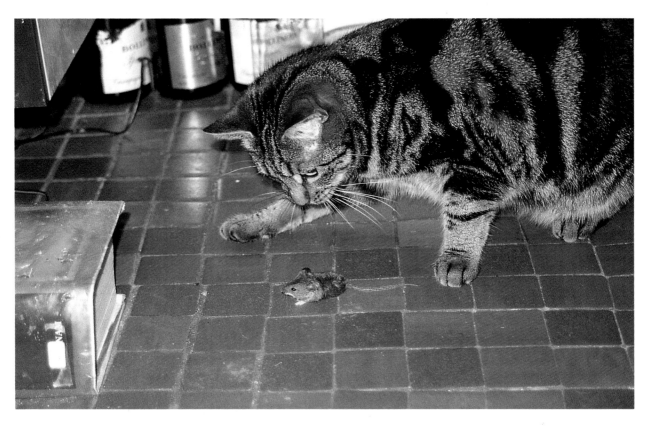

YOUR ATTITUDE TOWARD PREY

To shriek and behave badly toward the cat for what is a normal part of its behavior is, to say the least, a display of bad interspecies manners. It is kinder to the cat and your relationship with it to discreetly dispose of the prey. If the prey is still running around, remember that it will run alongside walls and not into the open. I have found that the easiest way to capture an elusive mouse or vole in such circumstances is to position strategically a prone boot and, when the fugitive has run into it, take it quietly outside and release it in an appropriate place.

encountered. In either case the hunter stands to lose its prey to others. Yet overriding this is the advantage of taking the prey out of its known area, tightly held in the mouth as first grabbed, and dropping it in the cat's own heartland, where it knows the runs like the back of its paw.

On releasing its prey, the cat is anticipating manipulating and dazing it fully so that it can be dispatched by the feline neck bite. However, the prey's prime need is to escape. Both are trapped in the survival ploys that best aid their species.

After stunning the prey, the cat cannot just finish it off because it may be "playing dead" (akinesis) and may turn and bite the cat as it tries to bite

the prey. So the cat feigns disinterest and looks about while waiting. This is what the prey has anticipated, and it makes a dash for safety. The cat wheels around and lands a paw again on the fleeing potential food. This is repeated a number of times, but not infrequently the prey reaches some cover and makes good its escape. So this apparent play is a macabre game that both stand a chance of winning.

Whenever a cat brings its prey back into the house, a number of things are happening. First there is the geographical advantage. Secondly, as in the feral state, the cat is also displaying to other "cats" that "this is a good place to be" by its actions. If the prey does escape, the cat is only "stocking its own larder," for a small mammal will normally not regain its own range for a long while. This is one good reason for farmers to have mainly female cats; males will bring in prey from the fields, while most prey catches of queens will have been in and around the barnyard, and an escape does not increase the inhabitants.

It can be a real problem when cats bring their prey back to old houses full of hidey-holes and then lose them. The prey are not usually house mice and so are ill equipped to survive house dwelling for long and can die marooned under a floorboard, leaving a telltale stench of death.

Another reinforcement to the cat in this behavior is that we are fairly hopeless "kittens," showing no signs of catching our own prey. Cats behave toward us in a mixed manner: frequently we are adults and they juvenile, but at other times the reverse, and sometimes the relationship is adult to adult or "kitten" to "kitten."

Cats and the Bird Feeder
To have a bird feeder in a garden that is frequented by cats may seem to be providing them with a stocked cupboard. But many people like me love to have both cats and birds about, and it is not as crazy as it sounds!

Cats rarely catch birds, in contrast to other prey. Both cats and birds are at a superabundance in suburban areas because we provide food and shelter to both. Not having a cat so that you *can* have birds, or vice versa, will not change the reality that in your neighborhood there are huge numbers of both.

I have had a bird feeder in my garden for years from which birds have successfully fed in numbers and been helped to overwinter successfully, and all without the avian equivalent of the "Slaughter of the Innocents."

It is possible to make your feeder less user-friendly to cats. Rustic wooden-legged tables allow the cat to sprint up them, while smooth metal poles do not.

It is also possible to have no pole and to suspend the feeder on chains. Poles can have a lampshade-like collar that opens downward, which is effective against cats. Some people like to keep out gray squirrels and pugnacious starlings as well as cats, and so use a roofed table with wire-netting sides or a similar restricted-access system.

I have been able to have coexisting cats by using a simple open table and

Cats catch far fewer birds than they do rodents and other small animals, yet we are often more emotional about their capture.

Opposite: A mouse is closely stalked in the quiet deadly game of cat-and-mouse.

paying attention to its siting. A potentially major problem with an open platform table is that if it is positioned anywhere near a fence or wall, cats can leap onto it. Placing it in the center of a vast expanse of lawn with nothing near is no alternative, for you will see very few birds. They need other birds about to convince them that all is well and that it is safe enough to feed. An isolated table will remain nearly bird free, while one adjacent to bushes on which birds can gather will see far more. I have found that having my feeder separated from the fence and a

tree by a japonica (flowering quince) works very well. It has a most attractive early and long-lasting flowering season, which is an asset to any garden, but it also has wicked spiny thorns that cats avoid but birds don't notice.

Many of the fears about cats and bird feeders are irrational, for in reality cats do not catch birds on feeders. Even if they can reach the platform, by the time they are on it the birds have flown. The worst that happens is that the cat just sits on the feeder for a while.

The real risk is that birds feeding on the ground are stalked by cats, so it is better to feed them on a table than on the ground and to try to prevent spillage from the feeder.

HUNTING

Cats hunt, catch prey, and eat it — they are carnivores. To expect them not to hunt is unreasonable both because of their biology and the natural order of things. Cats that catch birds cause cat-owning bird lovers much concern. Yet it is due to the privileged relationship that we share with cats that they bring a large proportion of their prey back home, and if they did not, far

fewer owners would have cause to worry. In the United States, where many cats are kept strictly indoors, their natural craving for raw meat is solved by including it in their diet.

Leroy, one of my cats, is a dedicated hunter, but he is typical in that his prolific catches reflect the richness of prey in the area he uses and the size of that area. I live in a water mill on a river, and there is an extensive rabbit warren a few hundred yards away. During the height of the young rabbit season, he brings one home every other day. Yet when we lived in a village, he did not catch one. There, thanks to a pond in the garden, he brought in many frogs but rarely killed them.

The availability and abundance of prey make a big difference. Leroy's catch in the village was much lower than it is at the mill. As a male, Leroy has a larger range than my female cat, which gives him access to a wider prey area. While the size of the range of rural feral cats reflects their prey requirements, prey is not necessary for the survival of domestic house cats; their range sizes are independent of the abundance of prey. While this could make them more of a danger to local wildlife, they are not, for a number of simple reasons.

First, not all house cats are competent hunters, and most catch prey only occasionally. Second, city cats catch only a fraction of what is caught by rural cats. I discovered this in my work with London's house and feral cats. Although cats are superb hunters, it is their strong scavenging ability that

Opposite: It could be a long wait for lunch on the bird feeder.

THE CAT'S EFFECT ON WILDLIFE

Cats have not been found to be endangering wildlife populations on continents (with the possible exception of Australia), but they have had a devastating effect on some island species. A number of island birds became extinct with the aid of the cat, such as the Guadalupe rufous-sided towhee, the Diffenbach's rail, and the Sandwich rail. However, in all but one case, the effect of the cat was part of a package in which introduced dogs, cattle, goats, rats, and people also had major involvement. Only in the most particular case of the Stephen's Island wren near New Zealand has a cat almost unambiguously pushed a species into extinction, when the lighthouse keeper's cat on the tiny island both discovered the species and took its catches back home. (However, even there, collectors were also involved in the bird's extinction.)

allows them to survive as feral-living animals and live with us eating food off a saucer. The urban feral cat seeks both "waste" food from plastic bags and garbage cans and food on a plate from feral feeders.

Third, contrary to common belief, cats do not catch many birds but mainly small mammals. Proportionately, town cats catch more birds than their country cousins. What is often overlooked is that although cats are far more common in towns than in the country, so are birds. As well as feeding cats, we also feed birds. We provide artificial nest sites in the form of birdhouses. Our gardens provide good habitats in the form of rich scrubland, with excellent insect support due to an increased flowering time in the year, and lawns with abundant earthworms. Our actions can be seen as providing optimum conditions to maximize bird numbers! Consequently, when Chris Mead of the British Trust for Ornithology assessed the numbers of ringed garden birds caught by cats, he found that cats were not having a harmful effect on bird populations.

Although many studies on what cats catch and eat have been made around the world, one by Bedfordshire schoolteacher Peter Churcher in Felmersham village caught international attention. Unfortunately, others made unreasonable interpretations from it, suggesting a "national carnage caused by cats devouring over seventy million individual prey."

The error arose by multiplying simplistically the annual catch of the average village cat, which was 14 prey, by the total number of cats in the country. Since most cats live in towns near people, in small ranges and with a fraction of the hunting success of rural village cats, the sum was meaningless. What is significant is whether the prey populations can sustain the predation. On most continents, prey species have survived the attention of cats for centuries. In Britain, both in Felmersham and nationally, cats cull only 5–6 percent of the annual productivity of the house sparrow — which is why house sparrows continue to thrive despite any feline presence.

The Effect of Prey on Predator

Although it might seem that all a prey species does for a predator is provide lunch, they do have a particularly linked relationship, but who controls whom? It might seem a strange question to ask, for historically human hunters just accepted that predators control prey numbers. However, in 1967 Paul Errington, who had written about the hunting of his cat in Wisconsin, suggested that in good habitat there is a "doomed surplus" whose loss does not affect prey density. It became realized that the number of predators was limited by numbers of prey, so ironically, prey controlled predators.

I believe that in reality it works both ways, depending on the circumstances. The particular significance of the cat in the equation is that although the completely independent feral cat living entirely on its catches on an uninhabited island is controlled by the interplay between these effects, other cats can step aside with different rules.

The house cat is completely supported by alternative food, so potentially would not be stopped from hunting a particular prey species out of existence locally. The urban feral cat's mixture of scavenged food and hand-outs similarly supports it. This could make the cat very damaging if it were not for the prey species, such as songbirds, also being supported.

What might at first sight seem simple is further muddied by the scavengeable food available to other predator species, such as foxes. Additionally, most predators have enough flexibility in their choice of prey species to shift to another when the numbers of one fall, so in that sense other predators are also supported. Consequently, we should not leap to conclusions about the damage

A cat stalks among the pigeons in Venice.

Opposite: Extinct Stephen's Island wrens; catalogued and cat caught.

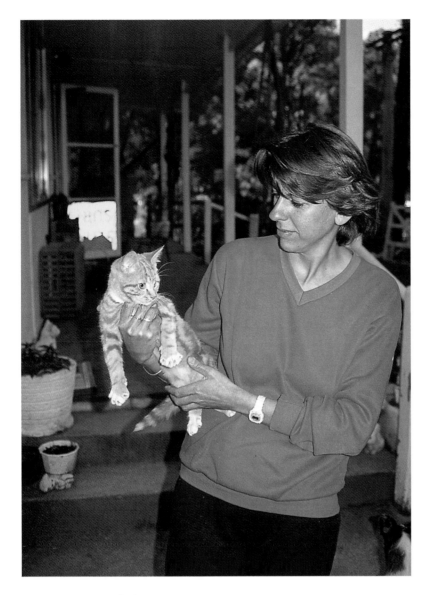

Some towns in Australia have introduced "cat curfews" when cats must be taken in for the night. However, the number of native animals caught by cats in urban and suburban Australia is minimal, as most have been displaced by habitat change.

competing with other predators, so the effect of the cat on kestrels, for instance, is unknown.

Cats with large ranges in rural areas are at lower densities and therefore have less impact on the local wildlife. As B. M. Fitzgerald, researching in New Zealand, has pointed out, at low densities cats may have little control on rats, which may themselves be damaging ground-dwelling species.

The Australian Dimension

The first British cats to arrive in Australia landed with the convict fleets at the end of the 18th century. By a century later, another introduced animal, the rabbit, had reached major pest proportions, and a widespread policy developed of breeding and releasing cats on farmland in an attempt at biological control of the rabbits. To an extent it worked, for in Australia cats eat more rabbits as part of their diet than anywhere else in the world. But the policy boomeranged as the special marsupial wildlife of the continent, previously isolated from placental mammalian carnivores, began to succumb.

A passionate debate has developed in Australia over cats, and although the cat *is* eating *some* native animals, it may be a scapegoat, for it is only doing so in the bush, since indigenous animals have been largely eradicated by farming in agricultural areas. Nonetheless, despite fierce opposition in 1995, South Australia passed a Draconian state bill specifying that *any* unidentified cat could be destroyed.

to wildlife populations by the cat.

That cats can undeniably control prey populations was found during World War II by C. Elton, who for national survival was investigating ways of reducing rat damage to stored grain in farms. Cats usually have difficulty in killing adult rats but are expert in catching youngsters. So if the farmer could reduce the adult rat population around his buildings, the resident farm cats were able to maintain that level by culling the youngsters.

Strangely, very little research has been carried out on the effect of predators

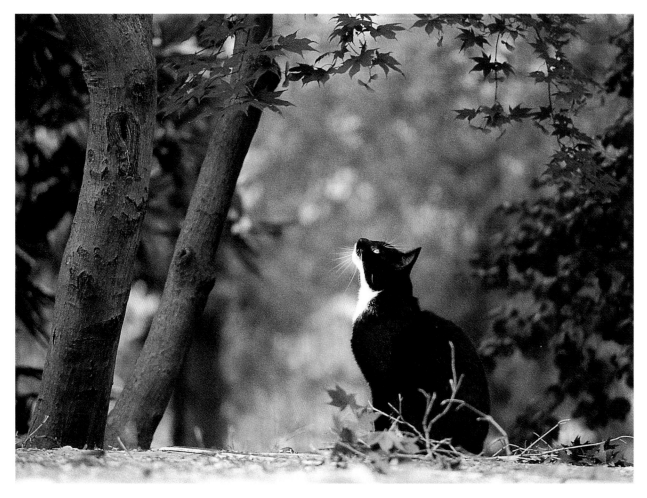

An American Civil War

A similar dispute has been raging in the United States, the largest cat-owning society in the world. There are now more cats than any other pet — more than 55 million — and there could be around 60 million feral cats. During 1993 and 1994 an alarming battle raged in the country over attempts to have a "feline fix bill" passed in the California state legislature in an attempt to reduce feral cat numbers; the assumption was that cats were having a devastating impact on American birdlife.

Yet it is too easy to blame the cat just because it is a carnivore, when other factors can be far more significant. Recent attempts in the United States to encourage the neutering of feral cats but to make it illegal to return them to site have demonstrated a lack of understanding of the effectiveness and advantages of neutering and returning them in producing a lower feral cat population. If cats are annihilating their prey species, the controls should be ones that work. Removing cats from where there was once a good population just buys a temporary respite until a new population develops.

A hunting feral cat watches for prey in Washington, D.C.

Preventing behavior problems

An indoor cat looks wistfully outside. Housebound cats are more likely to suffer behavior problems than those with access to the outside world.

There are three main "problems" that cause cat owners anxiety: fouling, aggression, and damage to furniture. Most "behavior problems" are not problems in themselves; it is where they occur that makes them problems — in the home. It is often just normal behavior in an inappropriate place — inappropriate for us.

The four main causes of the behavioral problems of cats can be grouped as confinement, stress, physical ailments, and early conditioning. Confinement and stress are the major problems.

Confinement

The single main reason for the great increase in behavioral problems over the last few years has been the increased number of cats that are kept confined. With the cat's range reduced to the size of the home, everything has to happen there, so the events that would normally be diffused over a larger area outside are focused on you and your home. Once cats are allowed outside to set their own territorial and range limits, most of the confinement problems disappear. The link between behavioral problems and confinement is something that zoo managers in particular have to address with regard to their caged animals.

Confining the independent cat with a heritage of 3,500 years in the outside world is bound to cause problems. We may feel safer inside our homes, away from the apparent risks of vehicles and disease, but we must be careful not to transpose our fears onto our cats when it is not necessary. However, if you live in a high-rise building in the middle of a busy city, the risks are higher than elsewhere. If you intend to keep a cat in a confined area, there are ways of circumventing problem situations.

Among domestic cats today, readily available food has already reduced the need for large ranges. But by confining cats, you are setting their range limits, so individual features of their reduced landscape become more important, and you in particular become the focus for play, hunting, and aggression. Not the least of the problems is that a trapped cat becomes a bored cat.

Although cats will adjust with time, I have found that if normally active indoor/outdoor cats are confined, over the first two weeks they become more overt and demanding. If more than one cat is confined, then the frequency of ambushes of one on another increases as the days go by.

If you live in an apartment two or three floors up from a garden, do not automatically assume that you cannot have an indoor/outdoor cat. In Amsterdam the back walls of many apartments have cat ramps of single planks with grip slats that enable the cats to go up a couple of flights. At my own watermill home my cats enter the building through a cat flap a couple of floors up.

Stress

A lot of neurotic behavior in a cat can be caused by stress, and that is often linked to density. Too many cats in a confined space can cause problems. This is often encountered by those who take far too many stray cats into their home to "save" them from the outside world. The pungent smell of cat spray and urine can often be overpowering in such a house.

Even if cats are unconfined, the introduction of yet more cats can cause a range of problems. Because cats recognize our place in their world, so the arrival of a new baby, new partner, or even a new neighbor with pets can cause them stress. For a cat not used to socializing, the sudden arrival of a lot of visitors at your home or the

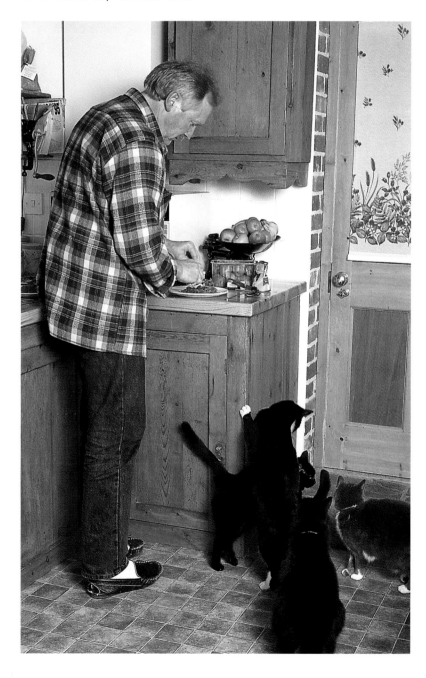

High cat densities can lead to stress problems, and aggression can become noticeable around mealtimes.

incarceration of the cat at the vet or cattery can also be stressful.

In response to stress, fouling can become a serious problem, and aggression can occur. The cat may begin overgrooming. It can undergo appetite changes, losing interest in food or overeating. It can also enter an anxious, depressed state, in which it may remain for long periods, hunched up with wide-eyed pupils.

EARLY CONDITIONING

The Antisocial Cat

If you have an antisocial cat that does not like people, it probably did not have enough human contact when it was a kitten. But if a social adult cat becomes antisocial, look for a reason for its change in behavior. It might be suffering aggressive attacks from a nearby dominant tom; it may have been left for a while at the vet for treatment; or it may have been hit by a vehicle. These are the type of events that can cause such a behavioral change.

The Socially Dependent Cat

If your cat has focused its attention on you alone since it was a kitten, this can cause particular problems if it is put into a cattery when you go away. Deprived of you and its home, it may become depressed, refuse to eat, and lose weight.

Don't Treat a Cat Like a Dog

Training a dog is relatively easy, but training a cat is totally different. The dog, with its open geography and hierarchical background operating within a group to hunt, is programmed to cooperate and obey a pack leader. The pecking order is sorted out before the hunt and established by aggression within dog society. We can fit into the niche of the dominant dog, and tell a dog what to do.

When a cat hunts, it does so alone, so cooperation via aggression does not occur and ordered instructions to a cat will have less significance to the animal. When cats do come together and form a group in a semi-social way, this behavior does not revolve around the hunt, and the interactions can be categorized as more affectionate than aggressive. Consequently, in your role as a type of cat in your "cat group," affectionate interactions will increase your reciprocal bonding with your pet. The simple aggressive dominance effective in dog training is therefore inappropriate for cats.

Although it is possible to establish relative hierarchies among a group of cats, it is less significant and of a lower key than in the dog world. It is possible to view an "acknowledgment hierarchy" in which the affectionate move of head rubbing may be initiated by a lower-ranking animal toward a higher-ranking cat more frequently than to a lower-ranking one. The parallels are the "fawning" appeasement moves of dogs.

Once you have trained your dog to carry out a command, it will continue to follow your instructions. You can tell a cat to "get down off that table" and to an extent it may do as you wish while you are around, but not necessarily when you have gone.

Active and Passive Deterrents

Passive deterrents work better in modifying your cat's behavior than active ones. You can fall back on active deterrents when necessary, but to avoid weakening your bond with your cat, it should not realize that you initiated them.

One of the simplest active deterrents is a ball of paper that you can lob at your cat if it is making mischief, but it must not be seen to come from you. It also has the decided disadvantage that your cat may think it a game and chase after it.

An old standby is the toy water pistol, which can be used when the cat is carrying out the act you wish to prevent. But again, it is vital that you are not seen to aim it at your cat; the water must seem to appear out of the blue. As a technique it should not be overused.

A method employed by animal behaviorists for certain situations uses an upside-down mousetrap. For example, a cat that repeatedly digs up a large potted plant can be dissuaded by this method. The trap mechanism is set and placed carefully upside down on the pot soil and covered slightly with a piece of paper and soil. When the cat starts to disturb the soil, the trap makes a noise. I am very wary of this method, for cats' paw bones are small and easily damaged. If you do employ this method, take extra care and use it only as a last resort.

Passive techniques are usually easier, both on your cat's and on your nerves, and do not jeopardize your relationship.

If a water pistol is used as an active deterrent, it is vital that the cat does not see it in use.

A handful of mothballs in a pierced plastic bag on the soil is one example, as naptha is toxic to cats. Cats dislike the smell — but so might your visitors.

The key passive techniques are best illustrated as alternative approaches to the main problem voiced by cat owners — fouling.

Avoiding the Mess by Passive Deterrents

Once a cat has started to urinate or defecate in your home, it will tend to return and use the same spot. It will detect a residual scent even after a reasonable cleanup, and the spot will seem like a safe latrine. So you need to be thorough. Among the range of disinfectants and bleaches available, avoid coal or wood-tar products, since these are known to have toxicity for cats. Similarly, avoid using ammonia-based products, as they will encourage urination because of their smell.

The recommended agents for areas used by cats are based on sodium hypochlorite. In the United States the most popular products include Out-Right, Nature's Miracle, and Nylodor. Check whether such treatment will damage fabric by trying a small hidden area first. Enzyme-containing biological detergents are also effective, and some are sold specifically for dealing with this problem.

Once the area has been made odor-free, you can change the geography of

Change the geography so that there is no room for a cat to reuse an inappropriate latrine site.

the room. You can put a group of ornaments or even empty milk bottles in the area so that there is not room for the cat to squat down and use it. An alternative is to unroll some aluminium foil and place it on the favored spot. Your cat will not like walking on this and so will avoid the location.

Fouling the Floor — Practical Considerations

While stress factors such as increasing the density of cats in a home can cause fouling, a number of other reasons within a household can also give rise to this problem.

The cat is the most fastidious of animals. No other domestic animal buries its feces. If a cat is confined and for some reason does not like the litter tray, then you will find mess around your home. Usually it is the owner's fault rather than the cat's because of a lack of litter cleanliness.

If a cat starts fouling, your first consideration should be whether you are changing the litter frequently enough. It is pointless to tell a cat off when you are leaving a litter tray uncleaned for two or three days. Cats vary a great deal over this. My cat Tabitha would much prefer to use a litter tray rather than the outside world. So when circumstances mean she has to use one, I could be slapdash and leave it for a number of days without it bothering her too much. Leroy, on the other hand, much prefers the garden and is so fussy that he will dig a number of holes before he is happy with the spot. He finds using a litter tray an indignity, so the thought of using even a lightly soiled one is an abomination.

A cat may also foul if it is trapped inside for a length of time. It does not have to be physically trapped for problems to occur. For a shy cat, noisy guests can make it feel trapped. A large increase in the number of local cats can cause a shy cat problems about "going" outside.

Other things can also shut your cat in. When a cat is elderly or infirm, very cold weather can make it think twice about going outside. For some cats, a thick layer of snow can blanket off the soil completely, and you may need to clear a patch for them or use a litter tray at such times to prevent problems indoors. During hot weather female cats with small ranges and a limited variety of places to dig may find the soil rock solid. They would welcome an occasional turning of an area for use.

In itself, this is usually not much of a problem, but when a particular stress problem exists, it may tip the balance.

Health problems can cause a cat to foul. A cat that suddenly starts to urinate around the house may not have a behavior problem but cystitis. Elderly cats may have not only arthritis but also a weakened sphincter muscle of the bladder and may not be able to reach the litter tray or the outside world in time. In this situation it is pointless to become cross with your pet.

Cold weather reduces the size of a house cat's outside range — and a layer of snow can dissuade some cats from finding somewhere outside to use as a latrine.

Fortunately, kittens take readily to using litter trays.

The Litter Tray

Cats rarely need initial training to use a litter tray, but if you do need to retrain your cat, it is usually a fairly simple procedure of putting it in a small room, preferably with floor tiles, such as a bathroom, and then introducing it to the litter.

At one time the only choices for litter were earth or sand, but now there is a wide range of commercially available litters with different characteristics, and at least one should suit your cat. Unfortunately, your cat may not like the one you find easiest to carry.

Some litters are made from wood fibers, some from corn husks, and some from clay. Behaviorally, I find the best litters are those that clump together on absorbing the urine and dry the feces, because they make the excreta easily removable on a daily basis. The litter will therefore be more acceptable to the cat because the odor is reduced.

Nonclumping litter will usually need more frequent changing or the use of a litter freshener — and overuse of that can be off-putting to some cats. Multicat households can present problems, as some cats find use of the litter by the other cats unnerving.

For cats that like a quiet corner, covered trays can be an advantage. For owners they also mean that litter is less likely to be scattered and that odors are more contained. Some covered trays even have flaps and air filters to minimize any impact.

Litter provides the owner of the indoor/outdoor cat with an occasional convenience when circumstances arise and also has allowed the existence of the American-led trend of keeping cats confined. In the United States the cat litter industry promotes the concept of the indoor cat. The downsides are the behavioral problems of the confined cat plus the ecological disturbances of the industry. The volume of mineral extraction alone is colossal. There is also a real health risk of toxoplasmosis damage to unborn babies if pregnant women come into contact with soiled cat litter. (Wearing rubber gloves can prevent infection.)

Spraying

Spraying around the house by cats should not be confused with urination. If a cat is leaving dampness on the floor within a corner of a room, it will be from urination, but if it has been left some way up against a jutting-out corner of a wall or piece of furniture, then it will be from spraying.

The intact tom will reverse against an object and with a quivering, vertical tail release a pungent spray that sends a powerful scent message. The neutered tom or queen can spray, but the event will be of a lower key and the cat will usually position itself less dramatically, nearer to a urination stance. Under stress a neutered tom can occasionally spray like an intact tom, but the liquid will lack the smell. The spraying of an intact tom has a territorial marking function, so to assert its right to be somewhere, it will repeatedly spray small but highly pungent volumes as it patrols.

Neutering is the simple answer for your cat if it is a spraying tom, and after about a month it should cease to be a problem in 90–95 percent of cases. Behavioral deterrents may be persuasive in the handful of cases that neutering does not control. If they do not work, then discuss with your vet the possibility of hormonal control.

If you are troubled by a prowling neighborhood intact tom that comes into your home and sprays, then change your cat flap to one with selective "keys" that are worn on your cat's collar.

Damaging Furniture

A major problem for owners of housebound cats is the damaging of furniture. Even cats allowed access to the outside world will damage furniture, although not as much. Cats need to scratch for a number of reasons, and your best defense is to provide alternatives. A rush mat on the floor will be readily used by some cats but not touched by others. In the outside world the most frequently used surface is the bark of a favored tree, so the fronts of the arms of armchairs are commonly used by cats as "trees." The cat will tend to use the same spot time after time, for one of the functions of clawing a tree is to leave a visual territorial mark. Consequently, to yell at a cat after you have allowed it to develop a regular scratching post is unlikely to be effective, as the cat is drawn to the

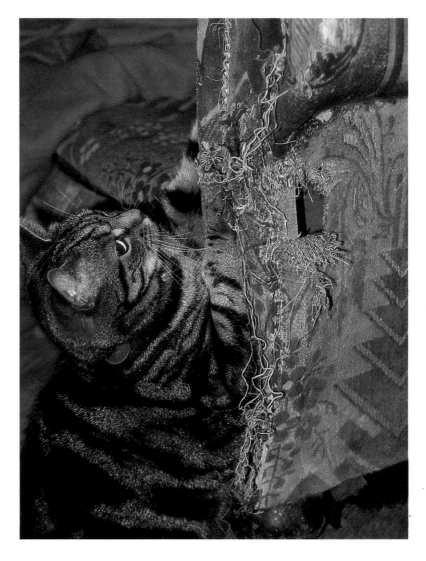

Once a cat has begun to cause damage to furniture, the "marking" it has made will attract it time and again to what it will come to consider as its "spot," and its repeated actions can cause severe damage over time.

The placing of alternative scratching "posts," such as rush matting, will help to prevent further damage to furniture around the house.

arms with other material or aluminum foil to put the cat off.

Then you need to redirect your cat's action onto a scratching post. Many of these are commercially available and are constructed with sisal twine, carpet, or a similar surface on a wooden post, but they are easy to make. If you have a cat from kittenhood, you should encourage it to use a scratching post. However, if a cat starts to damage a chair or table leg, then place the post directly in front of the position. Transfer your cat across onto the post when it attempts to claw the furniture, gently encouraging it to use the post instead.

Some people find the active deterrent of the water pistol useful when their cat is in the act of clawing the furniture — but remember the cat must not see it being fired.

Declawing is a truly barbaric, disabling mutilation and should not even be thought of as a means of control for this problem.

visible damage. You need to prevent it early on.

If the cat's favored scratching post is wooden furniture, you can rub on passive deterrents in the form of a strong-smelling polish or vinegar (check first that this will not damage the surface), which the cat will not like. You could place half an orange alongside the problem spot for the same reason. On padded furniture you can change the geography by covering the

Aggression

Aggression is probably the most common reason after fouling why cat owners seek out the advice of behaviorists. Yet aggression is not a straightforward problem to deal with, for it is a catch-all word used by owners for a variety of situations.

Even true aggression is colored by the context, for both an attacking and a defending cat in an encounter are behaving aggressively but in differing ways. Perhaps the most straightforward aggressiveness is that which I have monitored in kittens around five days old. With eyes yet to open but with sound perception developed and a keen sense of smell, young kittens in a litter at this helpless stage will open their

a new cat is introduced. This can be protracted if a proper introductory procedure is not followed. Remember that young animals will adapt more readily than adults. The introduction of

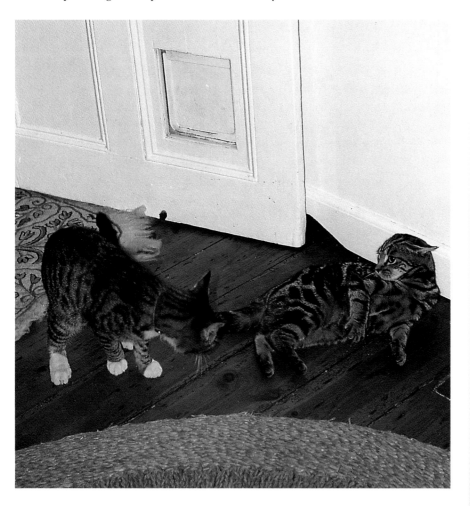

mouths wide and hiss at the smell of strange cats when their mother is away from the nest. This is an entirely appropriate response to an unknown world, and in understanding aggression we need to consider appropriateness.

Many cat owners are alarmed when their home becomes a battlefield between seriously sparring cats because

a kitten to a resident adult will be easier than the other way around. Similarly, when new cats move in next door, particularly if one turns out to be a wide-ranging tom similar to your own, then as the territorial geography is redrawn there will be aggressive disputes. How you react to your neighbors and their cats will affect how

Opposite top: Many owners find it alarming that while they are tickling their cat's tummy, it may suddenly grab hold and rake their hand with its back claws.

Opposite below: It is vital to spend time playing with your cat if it is housebound, to prevent it from becoming bored.

A cat "gym" provides a place where a cat can satisfy its tree-climbing instincts and generally "let off steam." Two cats will find a gym a great place for shared kitten games, even as adults.

your cats relate to the neighbors' cats. The dust should settle with a little time. However, do check your cat more regularly for signs of bites and scratches, which may develop into abscesses.

Even in more settled circumstances, in particular in high cat-density areas, if your cat is a queen, she may suffer the unwelcome attentions of a neighboring tom. While she associates with you as a member of your group, he believes her to be rightfully within his range of operations. This can lead to problems.

The situation usually occurs with intact toms, and you may be able to persuade your neighbors to neuter their cat. Failing that, the water pistol can be helpful, as can a cat flap with an individual "key" to provide a safe bolt hole for your pet.

Among indoor cats aggression toward you and your other cats can arise from boredom. Usually this takes the form of boisterous "teenage" games rather than real overt aggression and can be reduced by increasing play and interest in your cat's life by spending more time with it. Also give it somewhere it can be boisterous, such as a multilevel cat gym, where it can be harmlessly "arboreal," and remember to integrate it in play with your cat.

Attacking the Forearm

Many owners experience what they perceive as aggressive behavior suddenly appearing when they have been playing with their cat. The flip from play into this aggression is so sudden that they talk of it as schizophrenic behavior. What has happened is that they have been playing cooperatively with their cat when suddenly it grabs their wrist with its front paws, perhaps even attempting a bite, and vigorously kicks their forearms with its back legs. This is normal fighting behavior in which raking an opponent's belly with the back claws occurs.

Why it has occurred in this situation is that while the cat is playing happily, you have rolled it over onto its back and attempted to tickle its tummy. From

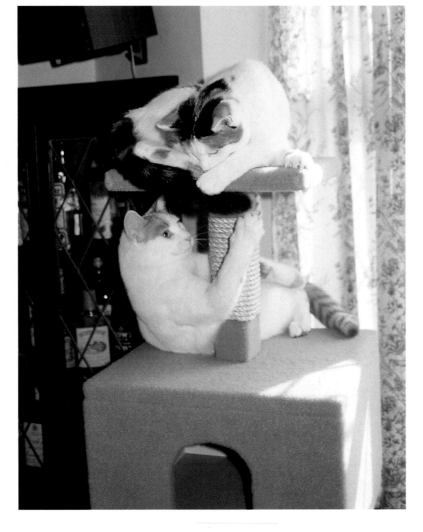

the cat's point of view, having had its
senses heightened, it suddenly feels
vulnerable. As your hand looms over, it
seems like a threatening cat, and your
pet is triggered into a response. (Part
sexual, part predatory elements are also
involved.) It is so easy to forget the
dramatic size difference between the cat
and ourselves, which makes even the
most confident of cats slightly wary at
times. The cat may learn to go into such
a move when our own movements are
more boisterous than appropriate.

What should you do? The first thing is
to stop moving and "play dead," and
the cat will stop and lose interest. Don't
pull your arm away, for this usually
increases the cat's actions. You may
need to distract the cat with your other
hand. Sometimes the use of a firm tone
can be helpful, but don't threaten to hit
your cat. Don't turn it into a game, or
the cat will keep repeating it.

Remember, you can anticipate the
event and avoid it by simply stopping
and standing up. You can restrict your
play so that you do not roll your cat
over. However, a fully trusting cat will
be happy to have its tummy gently
stroked by a friendly owner.

Breeds and Behaviorists

Understandably, far more dogs are seen
by behaviorists than cats, for aggression
in a dog commonly causes fear in
people and can lead to serious
problems, such as wounding or even
death. The link between temperament
and breed and type of breed in dogs
has been recognized in Britain by legal
restrictions on pit bull terriers.

In cats three or more toms are likely
to be seen by a behaviorist for every
queen as a result of territorial
aggression and spraying. It is notable
that half of the cats seen are breed cats,
although breed cats are only a small
percentage of the cat population. It may
be that breeds are more likely to have
problems due to their genes, and it may
also be that owners of breed cats are
more likely to seek help, but basically
the reason is the far greater tendency to
keep breed cats confined in the home.
Thus any of the breeds may exhibit
behavioral problems.

Keeping your cat healthy

THE HEALTHY CAT

The behavior of the cat we love can be changed by illness, overeating, being confined, and by its recent experiences. The imprint of its genetics and early conditioning are harder to modify, but the other causes can be addressed more directly. As a rule, proper cat care does make for an overall healthy cat.

Feeding Your Cat

When we feed our cats, it is a social event in which we interact together. This contrasts with the cat's solitary image, yet feral cats often take food back into their group's core area. Our own cats also regularly bring food back into the home. In that sense we are continually being a ready food source. As we bring back food for our cats, in large part we play the mother role and reinforce their "kitten" status. In another sense, as a continuing dependable food source, we are like a rabbit warren or garbage can around which cats can structure their ranges.

Small cats catch small prey and so repeatedly eat small amounts. When cats are given free access to food bowls they eat 10 to 20 times per day in small amounts. When we feed them twice a day and they rapidly devour the food, it is largely because of the way that we feed them.

That is not the entire story, though, for when cats have the opportunity to catch young rabbits, they will take advantage of the glut while it lasts. Although my cat Leroy may dispatch a two-month-old rabbit at one sitting, he usually eats half of a three-month-old the evening he catches it and the other half in the early hours of the morning, after a rest. This style of feeding on larger prey is not dissimilar to their usual feeding pattern in our households.

The Diet

You often hear "When I come back, it will be as a cat, for all they do is eat and sleep." Yet these two features of the cat's life are intricately linked. It is only because it eats the high-protein hunter's diet that it can invest in such a lot of sleep — around 18 hours a day either dozing or sleeping. This reduces stress and extends the cat's life longer than would be anticipated for an animal of

Left: Although cats are carnivores, they have a need occasionally to chew and swallow grass. Confined cats should be provided with grass in a pot or they will chew houseplants that may be toxic to them.

its size. But the cost to the kidneys of a high-protein diet is a continual barrage of toxic breakdown products. Kidney failure is a major cause of cat deaths.

The Need for Protein

As carnivores, cats have food requirements quite different from those of people. Don't ever think of making your cat a vegetarian, even if *you* are one. Apart from the immorality of imposing your whim as a flexible omnivore onto an obligate carnivore,

you will also kill your cat. The cat has a uniquely high requirement for protein, as it metabolizes both protein and fat rather than carbohydrate to produce energy. Cats need particular amino acids and fatty acids in their diet.

Cat-food manufacturers work to produce a well balanced diet in their complete products. (This is not always so in the gourmet ranges, so check on the label that it is a complete meal if you intend to feed your cat only on this type of food.) Often new flavors seem

OVERWEIGHT CATS

Our cats evolved as lone hunters that had to be in peak condition to survive, so they regulate their food intake. Unfortunately, we are not always helpful, for 1 in 10 cats in Britain and 1 in 3 in North America is overweight. We easily develop rituals of giving tidbits to our cats, which we find rewarding because it improves our social bonding. However, this does not usually cause cats to put on weight as much as overfeeding at mealtimes. We love our cats to love us, so we buy their favorite brand and ladle on that extra helping.

Many people who go out to work will leave extra food as a compensatory gesture to cover the guilt they feel for their absence. Far from being a kindness, this can lead to weight problems instead.

Multicat households are a real cause of uneven eating patterns. Some anxious cats are easily displaced from their food, while others are determined to eat anything in sight. You then have to resort to strategies such as feeding them in different areas. Do not leave the food of a "snacker" exposed if the household also has a fat "gorger."

aimed more at the purchaser's taste preferences than at the cat's, with combinations like salmon and shrimp when what a cat would prefer is mouse in a tin. Nonetheless, the balance in canned food aims at being similar to that of prey — around 75 percent water, with dry-weight measured components of 35 percent protein to 10–15 percent fat. Dry cat foods are used as a convenience, but they contain only around 10 percent fluid. Since the cat would normally obtain virtually all of its liquid intake from its food, unless it can compensate by drinking nearly a cup a day, the urine can become too concentrated, crystals form, and kidney damage results.

GROOMING YOUR CAT

The cat is the most fastidious of animals. Feral cats and many shorthaired house cats go through their lives without anyone grooming them but themselves, and they nearly always look immaculate.

The cat's tongue is covered with papillae, or spines, which make it a very efficient comb for grooming. During grooming, the cat also ingests vitamin D from its coat. This does not mean that you should not comb a shorthaired cat, but once or twice a week will be quite sufficient. Combing will enable you to check for fleas and to remove shed hair, so your furniture is less likely to end up looking like a yak. Combing will also mean that your cat ingests less hair and so is less likely to have hair-blocked bowels.

Longhaired cats fall into three groups.

First, the northern longhairs, including the Maine Coon and the Norwegian Forest Cat, have heavy coats. Second are the lighter-coated Angoras, Balinese, and Somalis, and third, the modern Persians. The natural coats do not need the intense attention that the modern Persian requires.

Breeding has modified the modern Persian's coat to such an extent that it is essential to brush and comb it daily. A modern Persian with a seriously knotted coat is a distressing sight, for the animal is unable even to walk properly because its skin is held taut in patches. This type of cat does not survive in a feral state. The older-style longhair-coated cats do not have the problems of the modern Persians. The traditional Angora undergoes a dramatic molt each spring, for its original home of Anatolia is freezing in winter and blisteringly hot in the summertime.

Modern Persians need gentle grooming from kittenhood so that they do not become agitated, but fortunately most have a good temperament and enjoy the attention. Ease out knots by using a wide-toothed comb or by hand. If the coat has become heavily knotted, seek a vet's help.

The buckled tear ducts of flatter-faced longhairs cannot drain properly, so fluid wells out of their eyes and mats the fur. Gently wipe with cotton, but avoid contact with the eyes.

The coat of longhair cats can become matted around the anus and infested with blowfly maggots in hot weather. Grooming is essential to prevent this.

Grooming a cat should become a pleasurable ritual for owner and cat alike and strengthen your mutual bond. It should never be a battle.

Fleas are more likely to reside where the cat finds it harder to reach with its probing, rough tongue. An urgent piece of washing usually indicates the presence of fleas; however, it can also be a habitual displacement activity, to cover that the cat is unsure of its next move.

FLEAS AND OTHER PARASITES

Grooming will soon tell you if your cat has fleas, if its scratching or sudden attacks of washing have not already alerted you. Comb your cat on some white paper, and if characteristic black specks appear, you have found flea droppings. If your cat has fleas, so does your house, and both will need treating.

Fleas are host specific, but if for some reason a cat is away for some weeks, they will make a desperate attempt at feeding on us. The fleas lay their eggs on carpets, bedding, or crevices in the floor as readily as on the cat. Warm summers and central heating boost their numbers.

At one time the California
approach to cat-flea "plagues" in a
hot climate was the electronic collar
sound system (right). The more
effective flea-control product
Program is now in use
nationwide in America.

Roundworm

Tapeworm

The vacuum cleaner should normally contain the flea problem around the house, augmented with an antiflea house spray. For the cat, flea collars are helpful but should not be used on kittens. Examine the neck area a few days after introducing your cat to a flea collar, as the skin of some cats has an inflammatory reaction to them. Insecticidal sprays and powders are effective, but many cats find the hissing from a spray unnerving, so a pump action may be better. Sprays and powders kill only the fleas on the cat at the time. As flea eggs hatch, the cat will need re-treating. Oral dosing of the cat to control fleas is becoming popular, as is the treatment involving a drop of a particular insecticide applied at the back of the neck, where the cat cannot reach, and absorbed into the body.

Some cats develop a flea allergy, and the animal's repeated washing of the affected area worsens the situation. This may need veterinary attention.

Cats can develop tapeworms from catching prey, but the most common tapeworm, *Dipylidium caninum*, can also be caught by a cat swallowing a flea during grooming. Although the immediate host is normally a rodent, this parasite's eggs can be eaten by the flea larvae and then taken up by the cat.

OTHER COAT AND SKIN PARASITES
Ticks

About 80 percent of ticks found on an afflicted cat are around the ears. Vets often recommend that you apply alcohol or insecticide before removing the parasite. Use tweezers to remove it cleanly, taking great care to pull vertically so that the mouth parts are not left in the skin; otherwise, an abscess will form.

Ear Mites

These minute animals are the most common cause of problems in the cat's external ear and will spread to other cats and dogs. Kittens are particularly vulnerable, and a plug of brown wax caused by a large number of mites can form in the ear. Vets will prescribe ear-drops, and treatment is essential; otherwise, a secondary infection can cause further damage to the cat's ear. Regular treatment at a time when the young cat needs to develop confidence with its new owner is behaviorally unfortunate.

Harvest Mites ("Chiggers")

The tiny red dots moving around on the cat's legs, feet, head, and ears in the autumn are harvest mites, which can cause irritation. Use flea spray to kill them.

Fur Mites ("Walking Dandruff")

This is normally spotted when the cat is seen to have dandruff on its back. Fortunately the mites are not common, as people can become accidental hosts. The mites can be treated with flea spray.

Lice and their eggs

Lice are uncommon in healthy cats, but they can be found on sickly animals. The eggs ("nits") stick to the fur and look like fine dandruff. They are controlled by flea spray.

INTERNAL PARASITES

An active hunting cat will pick up internal parasites from an intermediate host, such as a rodent or bird. While grooming your cat, you may find evidence of a tapeworm in its intestines from what looks like grains of rice in the coat. More disturbing to most owners is the appearance of a small, flat, white, moving creature in the fur near the cat's rear end. These are motile segments broken from the end of the tapeworm inside the cat.

The hunting cat can also pick up roundworms. Kittens can be infected during birth. You may find roundworms when your cat brings up a hairball. You should obtain courses of treatment for tapeworm and roundworm from your vet.

Toxoplasmosis

Toxoplasmas gondii is a single-celled organism that has the cat as its primary host. With the growing tendency to use cat litter, its life cycle needs to be understood because of the potential risk to unborn children.

Cats can be infected with the organism by catching prey. We can be infected by eating and handling raw or undercooked meat or by not washing our hands after gardening or playing with dirt. An infected cat will shed oocysts in its feces. These can be picked up directly by another cat and infect it, or they can be picked up by any bird or mammal — which includes us.

In most people infection may not have much effect, but in those with reduced immunity it can be serious. For

Top and middle: During a health check a vet listens to heartbeat and breathing, then examines the mouth and teeth.

Bottom: Wrapping a cat in a towel makes it easier to administer a pill by yourself at home.

an unborn baby with an undeveloped immunity, there is the risk of stillbirth, mental retardation, and blindness.

Cats are fastidious in their cleaning, so there is little risk of infection from handling them, but it would be safer for pregnant women to avoid contact with soiled cat litter. Use disposable gloves or, better still, get someone else to be responsible for changing the litter. If the litter is changed daily, the oocysts will not become infective in that time, so the risk is greatly reduced. Other than in warm climates most people are infected by undercooked meat rather than directly from feces in soil or litter.

CAT EQUIPMENT

Cat Flaps

For a cat to have its own door to a building is not a modern idea. I live in an ancient water mill that has had a cat hole in its door for hundreds of years for the working cats.

Today's cat flaps are an excellent development, for the flap keeps out cold drafts as well. Unfortunately, the simple flap can allow neighboring cats access if they know how to use flaps and are determined to enter. The scent of your own cat on the flap is usually enough to inhibit entry. If you are troubled by other cats, there are the additional options of a simple magnetic release or an electronic cat flap. Both allow access only to those cats with a magnet or color-coded collar tag.

Training for the Cat Flap

Some flaps open only one way and are not transparent, so the cat has to learn

to flip it up and work its way under it. Most, though, are two-way, so all the cat has to do is push. If the flap is transparent, the cat can check if it is safe to go through.

Whether the flap is one-way or two-way, initially it should be held wide open either by tape or a clothespin high up on the flap's side. Allow your cat to familiarize itself by sniffing the opened cat flap first. Encouraging the cat to pop through a few times by calling it is usually sufficient. Over a number of days, gradually lower the flap until there is only about a 3-inch gap and the cat has to push the flap to get through.

Once the cat is coping with that, drop the flap completely, and the cat will usually manage to open it. If the flap is either magnetic or electronic, the triggered locking device is usually better taped down or switched off while the cat is learning to use the flap. Once the cat is confident about using it, you can bring the selective device into operation.

Cat Collars

If your cat is an indoor/outdoor cat, it will need to have some form of identification. The simplest is the cat collar with a small name tag with your cat's name, your surname, address, and phone number. If your cat gets injured or strays, it is vital that you can be contacted.

A name tag also means that your cat is unlikely to be rounded up as a stray, or mistaken by a not-so-near neighbor who might otherwise assume it was homeless. Toms may have more than

124

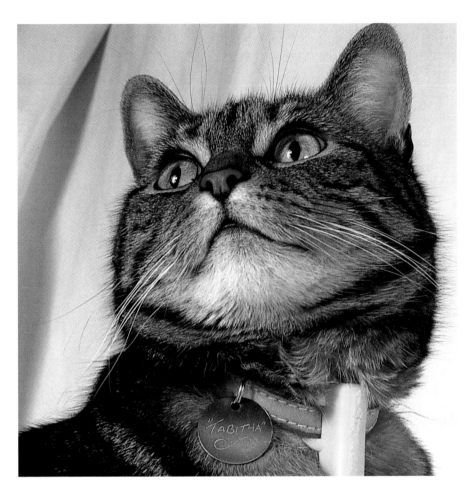

VACCINATIONS

Two vaccinations are currently routinely given to cats against feline infectious enteritis (FIE) and "cat flu" respiratory disease (feline viral rhinotracheitis [FVR]) and feline calicivirus disease (FCD). Once the passive immunity received by kittens from their mother's milk fades, it is important that they be treated. Your vet will advise you on timing. For show cats and any cats spending time in a cattery, it is essential that they receive their injections.

In those countries where rabies exists, it is advisable for your cat to have inoculations against it.

This cat wears its name and address tag, night-reflective collar, and color-coded "key" for its magnetic cat flap.

one "owner," since they range across a number of gardens and may be fed at more than one house.

A collar must have an elastic part so that if it is snagged, the cat can pull itself free. If it is fitted too slackly, snagging on tree branches becomes more likely. There should be just room for two fingers under the collar. If your cat is likely to walk across a road at night or even dusk, a reflective collar makes it more likely to be seen.

A very few cats manage to make a habit of catching a tooth on their collar, and for them the injectable identity microchip is an option.

Cat Leads

There will be times in all house cats' lives when the use of a lead and harness is invaluable. It is especially useful after you have moved and are introducing your cat to the "new" outside world. When buying a harness, make sure it is big enough and has a figure-8 design.

Many cats initially attempt to wriggle or squirm out of a harness or just flump straight down onto the ground. Since you will not want your cat to run off in a panic in an unknown place, it is vital to allow it to become used to the harness indoors. Let your cat wear the

Below is an injector "gun" and reader for the identity microchip. The chip is encased in a transparent block only so that it can be seen more clearly for the photograph.

Cat doors are not new. This cat is using the forerunner of the cat flap in the door of a historic water mill, provided to give access to the working cats of long ago.

Opposite: To introduce a cat to the garden of its new home, allow it to investigate on a long lead.

harness without the lead for a while at first. Lengthen the time it wears it, then connect the lead but allow it to remain slack and preferably do not hold it at the beginning.

If you drop the lead accidentally when you are with the cat in an unknown or potentially dangerous place, do not shout or charge after it, for this usually encourages it to run from you. It is far better to walk quietly and gently alongside the cat without looking as if you are about to pounce, and pick up the lead without a fuss.

TRAVELING WITH YOUR CAT

Cats can become stressed very easily when traveling by car and may call out repeatedly. They may work themselves into a state and be sick in only a few miles. In hot weather it is particularly bad for cats to become stressed in cars.

To prevent these problems, it is vital to condition your cat gently to travel, preferably from a young age. First make sure your cat is happy to use a carrier, or it will probably struggle as you approach with it in your hand, especially if you use it only when you visit the vet. Ideally, the carrier should be a ventilated plastic one that gives the cat a feeling of security and of not being exposed on all sides. Wicker carriers are not necessarily very secure or easy to clean.

Put in some newspaper, which cats

love to sit on, and gently put your pet in but don't shut the door. Leave the carrier around the house for some days so that the cat can use it as a nest. From time to time, walk the cat around the house in the carrier.

Initially, put the cat in its carrier into the car and sit with it there. Do this for a few days, then again with the engine idling. Introduce the cat to very short journeys and progressively longer ones. Be sure to drive smoothly and not too fast for the first few miles of the journey. Highways are generally easier for the cat because they have fewer curves and junctions.

For too many cats, the only journeys they make are to the vet or a cattery, which gives negative reinforcing. Because on some occasion you will probably have to carry your cat in an injured or seriously ill condition to your vet, it is important not to add unnecessary stress because you have not habituated your cat to travel.

Moving

Moving is a very stressful time for people, partly because of the separation and loss of a familiar place, friends, and memories, and partly because of the trauma of the upheaval and the arrival of the unfamiliar. It is the same for our cats. We at least know why the upheaval is taking place, but for the cat it is just perturbing.

Do not consider your cat at the last moment, but put it into a quiet room while the rest of the house is being emptied. If the cat has been scared and has run off at your old home, you can

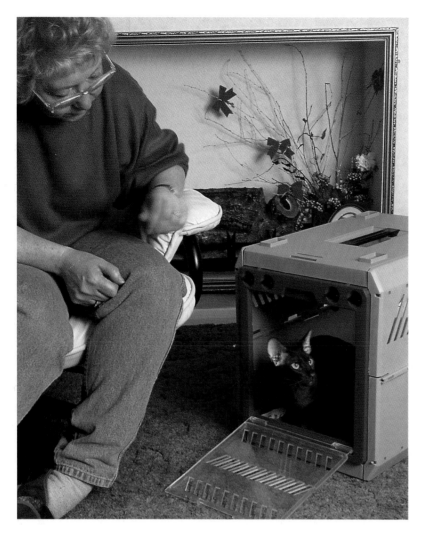

Introduce your cat to a cat carrier so that it becomes familiar with it before you need to use it.

sit and await its return. At the new home, no risks should be taken.

Take the cat in your car in its carrier to your new home and put it into a room where it will not be disturbed. Provide some food, a litter tray, and lots of reassurance. If the rest of the house is in a more settled state on the following day, begin to allow the cat to investigate. Do not allow the cat into the outside world for at least a week.

When you do allow your cat out for a brief sortie, it is safer that you take it on a harness and lead. Certainly, ensure that you remain near the cat's entrance back to its new home at first so that it becomes familiar with its safe return route. Do not leave the cat

outside alone but stay quietly with it. Gradually lengthen the time outside, and you will be able to gauge when it can be allowed to look after itself by its growing confidence.

THE ELDERLY CAT

Cats wear age with great dignity. My own old female cat, Mr. Jeremy Fisher, familiar to readers of my book *The Wild Life of the Domestic Cat*, reached almost 25 years of age. She remained remarkably fit, and until just a few months before her death, still walked along the top of the garden fence.

Intact toms can expect to live at least two years less than neutered toms. Neutering queens has little effect on their longevity. While 12 to 14 years is a good age for a neutered cat, male or female, few will live above 16. Some exceptional examples, like Jeremy, will make it into their twenties.

As the cat becomes less active, you may need to trim its claws more frequently. Its walking may become stiffer and the coat less lustrous. Nonetheless, it will still enjoy life, particularly snoozing in the sun.

You should pay particular attention to the cat's teeth and gums. If it does not stress the cat, cleaning the teeth can be helpful. If tartar builds up, gums become inflamed (gingivitis). Your vet can remove the tartar, or the teeth may become infected and be lost. Giving the cat some real meat to chew on occasionally can help it to clean its own teeth, which canned food cannot do.

The most usual cause of weight loss in the elderly cat is partial kidney failure. It may drink more. The cat's high-protein diet makes its kidneys particularly vulnerable. Consult your vet to see if this is the cause of your cat's weight loss. Some cats respond to treatment and a modification of diet for a while. The cat will retain a reasonable quality of life, but the point will be reached when this cannot be ensured. You should then discuss with your vet the realistic quality of your cat's life and what it can expect.

Euthanasia

Your pet will have become a loved member of your family and may well be your closest companion, so your grief will be real if it has to be "put to sleep." Your vet will appreciate your dilemma and advise you accordingly. But it is your pet, and the final decision will be yours. Discuss with the vet whether the act should take place at your home or in the surgery.

Normally, pet cats are put to sleep with an injection of barbiturate. You will also need to discuss with your vet whether you wish your cat to be buried in your garden or buried or cremated at a pet cemetery, rather than being disposed of in a more routine way.

Around 3 percent of all veterinary consultations involve euthanasia. These can be upsetting for the vet as well, despite being routine. Courses in bereavement counseling are becoming normal practice in veterinary schools.

An elderly cat, almost 25 years old, basking in the sun. Despite showing weight loss due to advanced kidney damage, it still enjoys snoozing in a favorite spot.

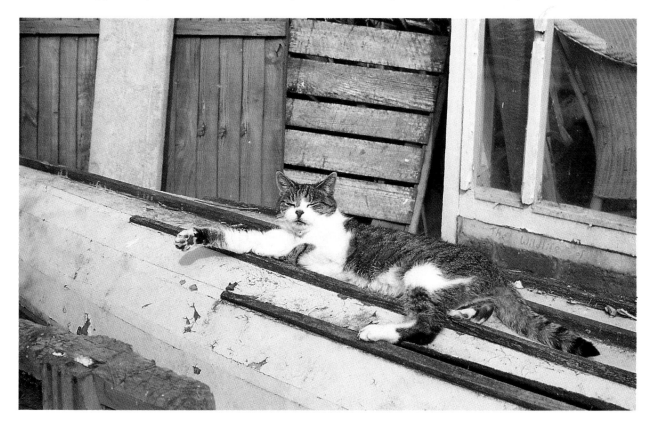

Life with our cats

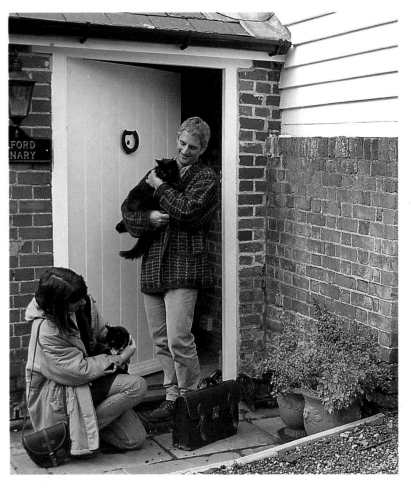

A young professional couple say good-bye to their cats as they leave for work. Cat owners acquiring a second cat to keep the first company when they are out has been a major reason for a recent massive growth in the number of cats owned in Britain and America.

THE SUCCESS OF THE CAT

Along the domestic route cats have engaged in a trade-off in which, overall as a species, they have done spectacularly well. Those that could initially tolerate being near people and their artifacts had access to a superabundance of food, which enabled their numbers to soar. Their distribution by people around the globe led to large localized islands of populations in and around urban centers, which enhanced a growing genetic diversity augmented by natural and artificial selection. Starting from a small population in the Middle East, cats are now spread worldwide in astronomical numbers that would normally be denied to any other wild predator.

On the downside have been the witchcraft era (see pp. 29–30), current breeding trends that have disadvantaged cats, and stresses caused by the recent trend to confine cats. High suburban cat densities increase the probability of feline fighting and traffic accidents.

Anthropomorphism

Throughout history, our continuing relationship with the cat has been obviously colored with anthropomorphism more than our relationship with any other animal. The cat has had its deified Egyptian ups and its 16th- and 17th-century European downs. Habituation was led by French aristocrats, writers, and actors. The early years of the cat fancy were assisted by two artists, Harrison Weir and Louis Wain. Showing cats promoted them as pets. But what is a pet? Wain's anthropomorphic portrayals of cats, in which he showed fluffy dressed Persians, blurred the line between cats and people.

Today many people are uneasy about the desirability of showing cats, for they believe that an animal that prefers territorial confidence should not be displayed alongside others. As in the argument against zoos, it is suggested that television and books keep the cats' positive profile high. Although my TV *Cats* series has now been shown around the world, when it was made, its documentary format for cats was an unusual venture for television. Showing remains a showcase for cats, and the fierce anticat lobby in parts of Australia and North America demonstrates the need for exhibiting the cat positively. Unfortunately, showing by its very nature promotes the breed cat over the moggie.

In Britain, there are two major cat shows each year — the National and the Supreme. At the latter, as well as showing the cats, there is a competition for the best-decorated cage. To some, the turning of an exhibition cage into a stage set is a harmless bit of fun and makes the cat's cage less austere. To critics, it seems as if the cage is a doll's house and not far from making Wain's dressed-up cats a reality.

Cats and Writers

The popularizing of the cat by writers and artists such as Edward Lear and Beatrix Potter has made them endearing images for children's pets. Edward Lear was so devoted to his cat Foss that when he moved, his new villa was constructed exactly like his old house so as not to inconvenience his cat in any way.

Not wishing to inconvenience the cat is common to many writers, though not usually on such a grand scale. The list of writers who wrote with their cat as companion ranges from the worthy Sir

Walter Scott to the scary Edgar Allan Poe and from the catlike Colette to the macho Ernest Hemingway. Many, including myself, will write around the cat rather than disturb it. Why do we do this, and what is the basis for the cat's special relationship with writers? Writing is a solitary profession carried out quietly, often at home, making the writer an ideal focus for the cat, while

The blurred reality of anthropomorphism: me and cat, with young women dressed up as cats, "borrowed" from the stage musical *Cats*, at the launch of my BBC TV series *Cats*.

A cat makes an ideal companion for the retirement years.

the cat is an ideal companion for the writer because it likes to sit and sleep beside you for hours. This behavior is equivalent to related feral cat group members sitting alongside each other or cats that sit together on the sofa for hours. These restful, nonthreatening sessions reinforce group bonds and assure the occupation of a key part of a range. Yet it becomes a time of apparent communion and empathy to the writer and cat as they are wrapped in contemplation. Small wonder the cat developed powerful friends among artists and writers who turned around the public hatred of cats.

While anthropomorphic attitudes can be derided, they are at the center of our relationship with cats, and behaviorally in many ways we relate to cats as if they were children. Yet anthropomorphism is a two-way street;

perhaps we need a different term to describe when cats behave toward us as if we were cats (feliomorphism?). We both recognize the other as a different species but behave as if we are not at the same time. Honorary people and honorary cats.

Cats fulfilling the role of perpetual children are responding to a growing need to bring contentment to an ever-increasing population of lonely, elderly people and nondemanding companionship to the large numbers of single people and single-parent families. Over the last decade cat ownership has increased dramatically by a third in both Britain and the United States. One of the main reasons for the increase is that young professional people are choosing to have cats instead of dogs because they are less restrictive and often serve as child substitutes while their owners delay having a family. With both partners out at work, the owners commonly feel that their cat needs a companion; hence the massive increase in two-cat households.

While some adore the cat as a dependent toy, fortunately others still love cats for their free-living spirit — the cat as cat.

Changing Attitudes Toward Cats

American attitudes toward cats are changing. Fifteen years ago most cats in North America, as in Britain today, were indoor/outdoor cats. Today more and more cats and their owners live in crowded urban settings — in apartments and homes. Thus more and more cats remain indoors. The hazards for cats are traffic death, urban predators such as raccoons, toxins used in lawn and garden treatments, and risk of disease. In Baltimore it was found that a cat had a 1 in 10 chance of being killed in a year on the streets. Where traffic is dense there is reason to be cautious. Disease risk figures are often expressed in the United States even though preventive injection courses exist. Rabies is endemic in the States, but the main risk of the disease is from dogs. Cats rarely communicate rabies.

Before keeping a cat confined, you need to weigh the possibility of disease risk and road death with the probability of confinement behavioral problems. Now the United States has a behavioral disaster, as most of the 55 million owned house cats are confined. Urinating around the house, "clawing the drapes," and aggression are now

significant parts of the American cat's lifestyle.

Alarmingly, at a recent meeting of American cat welfare organizations, one senior executive said, "Now I assume that one thing we can all agree about is that all cats should be kept in all the time?" How has this happened in the land of the free? Influential breeders and writers such as Milan Greer

A kitten undergoes a declawing operation in the United States.

promoted the idea of confinement in the 1960s. Ironically, the old natural breed of which America is rightly proud, the Maine Coon, developed as a robust cat because of its outdoor barn life.

Confined cats cause "problems," and owners often seek drastic remedies. Although declawing is justified as being a last-ditch stand against aggressive or furniture-damaging cats, it can be the first resort and carried out by vets on kittens. Although a caring and original writer, Greer recommended declawing, but he did at least argue that cats should be given the benefit of the doubt up to eight months of age. This

You can pour out your heart to your cat — and you can trust that your secrets are safe. A boy cuddles his cat in New England.

barbaric, unnecessary operation has become common in the United States. This mutilation of millions of cats is a real cost that needs considering when policy statements are made by welfare groups about captive cats. Fortunately, the British Veterinary Association and the Royal College of Veterinary Surgeons are firmly against declawing, and consequently it is not allowed in Britain.

Behavioral approaches are far better, and today practicing cat behaviorists are often available for consultation via veterinary referral.

The Temperament in the Cat–Human Relationship

Obtaining a cat "just happens" for most of us. A fifth of the population of house cats walked in off the streets. Some people are given pets; others inherit theirs when family members move or die. The majority seek out their cat as a kitten, either from someone with a litter or from somewhere like a Cats' Protection League shelter. The CPL, the largest charity in the United Kingdom concerned solely with cat welfare, annually finds homes for over 75,000

cats but handles more than double that number each year. A minority of people seeking cats want particular breeds and so visit a breeder.

Cats have individual characteristics, and one type will suit you better than another. Among breed cats, if you want primarily a lap cat, Persians tend to be more placid, while oriental cats, particularly Siamese, are outgoing. If you are choosing a moggy, look more carefully at the individual. When obtaining a kitten, select carefully. Remember, this relationship may last longer than many human ones — so give it more than a few moments' thought. Intriguingly, the feature that people normally use to select cats, regardless of behavior, is color.

Check that the kittens have been habituated to people. When making your choice, see how they respond to you. Appearance can matter, but so can behavior. Kittens played with by a number of people become less scared of people generally. Early handling habituation was an enabler during the early period of domestication, when little systematic genetic selection toward tractability occurred.

It is not unusual that a cat has become primarily attached to one person but has remained shy of other people. Do not despair; the cat can be changed by greater habituation to people in adult life and will improve, although its die is cast.

A cat's behavior can be modified, even though the sensitive period is long past. You can increase the bond with your pet. Don't just feed your cats, but spend time with them, so that each day you enhance the link.

Cat Communication

Our relationship with cats is two-way. Since we are two different species, it is remarkable that we can communicate at all. Our historical relationship with dogs is instructional, as they are a pack animal and we can elicit a trained response. In contrast, the independent cat does not usually play that game. However, in our shared lives the mutual responsiveness between people and cats is based on certain understanding and expressions of intent that are communicable.

Mildred Moelk in 1944 distinguished 16 utterances in the adult cat that she found imparted specific meaning.

The "song" of caterwauling is made by two facing cats, usually males making saber-rattling threats. Because of the high density of cats in suburban areas, town dwellers will have their sleep disturbed by caterwauling more than people who live in rural areas.

The shrieks, screams, and snarls of the active fight are also unambiguous. Cats have a melancholy distress howl, too. The distinguishing vocal feature between the small cats and the big cats is that small cats scream and big cats roar. This difference was believed to be the result of the hyoid cartilage being bony in small cats and flexibly cartilaginous in the big cats. Recently, however, it was discovered that the big cats have a large pad of elastic tissue connected to the upper part of the vocal cords allowing the roar to fully develop, a feature missing in the small cats.

Most of the cats' vocalizations that we hear are lower key. Some cats are very insistent with their request "meows" toward feeding time, while others remain mute. When cats greet each other or us, they will make a rising trill as they arch their back a little and bounce lightly on their front paws. As we walk toward the house, they will greet us in this manner or rise up to rub their head or mid-back against our hands.

Cats appreciate that our world is vocal and turn up the volume in comparison to the sounds made among feral cats. There has been positive feedback. They find that when they call, we pay attention. Similarly, they sit in front of a door, and we let them out. The communication is certainly two-way, so we do train each other into repeated patterns of behavior. We both reinforce our approval, for we stroke the cat's back, and it rubs around our legs.

We seem like large mother cats to our pets, and they purr contentedly. Sitting together we relax, and our stresses fade away.

Cat communication between mother and kitten is gentle in contact and sound, and purring bonds them perfectly.

Purring

The most catlike of all sounds is the purr — it is in essence feline. It is at the heart of our close relationship with the cat. Despite this, there are very few early historical references to purring in contrast to other feline features, such as the shining eyes. One does occur in the eulogy to Beland written by Joachim du Bellay in the mid-16th century:

> *He was my favourite plaything*
> *And not forever purring*
> *A long and timeless*
> *Grumbling litany.*

When purring is written about by authors, it gives an indication of the closeness of a relationship, as it generally occurs at times of affection. The fear of cats that stalked peoples' minds for centuries, putting the cat in league with the devil, prohibited any intimacy with them. Cats were kept to the utilitarian task of rodent control of barnyards. Clare Necker drew attention to the lack of an ancient Greek or Latin word for *purr*, which is consistent with our understanding that they did not keep cats as close pets.

Remarkably, there is still debate about how the purr originates. One idea was that blood surging through the inferior *vena cava* produced a sound as it forced its way past the central tendon of the diaphragm. It is now generally agreed that, like most vocalizations, the purr originates in the larynx. Muscles cause the vocal cords to close until air pressure forces them open. The involvement of the false vocal cords seems probable, as vets can prevent the problem of purring drowning out all other sounds on their stethoscopes by gently squeezing the larynx, which inhibits the false vocal cords while leaving the inner vocal cords unaffected. The diaphragm is also involved, as its rhythmic tensioning is essential for air control of the larynx. Indeed, purring is the "purrfect" cure for hiccups. Hiccups are caused by involuntary spasms of the diaphragm, and the tensioning of the diaphragm muscle during purring stops that.

A cat on our lap being stroked purrs in contentment. Yet before the close relationship of domestic cat and mankind, small felids were making the sound. It is the singularity of purring that makes it such a significant sound. It fulfills a role that is important to the cat family and particularly to the small cats.

To understand why our cats purr, it is necessary to ask why most other animals do not. What is it about the cat's way of life that makes it so vital?

However, purring is not completely exclusive to cats. Hyenas and viverrids are the closest relatives of the cat family, grouped together as the Aeluroidea, the catlike animals, and some make a sort of purr on suckling. Generally, across the three families, the animals tend to be solitary hunters and nocturnal.

When your cat purrs and kneads upon your lap, it is behaving toward you as if you were its mother. This fact was noted by Charles Darwin in 1872 in *The Expression of Emotions*:

Now it is very common with young cats, when comfortably lying on a warm shawl, to pound it quietly and alternately with their fore feet; their toes being spread out and claws slightly protruded, precisely as when suckling their mother. That it is the same movement is clearly shown by their often at the same time taking a bit of the shawl into their mouths and suckling it; generally closing their eyes and purring from delight.

Leyhausen believed that the function of purring was a signal from the suckling young to their mother that all was well. Once in the feline repertoire, purring could be used by a mother to reassure the young during suckling. However, many animals suckle but do not purr. In

During suckling, both mother and kitten will purr.

A cat displays a defensive, hissing snarl. In the defensive cat the pupils open wide, while those of the aggressor are in a tight slit.

Opposite top: The extreme arched position of the young agouti cat in Thailand combines features of both a defensive posture and one that threatens attack. Inexperienced youngsters will adopt it as a "safeguard" pose that they can develop either way.

Opposite below: The role of aggressor and defender is often more fluid than it seems, but here the closed pupils give a certain menace to the fistful of flick-knives.

kittens purring starts when they are about a week old. Before that age their limited movements do not seem to require the mother to hear the signal. Unlike sounds using the true vocal cords, the purring arising from the false vocal cords can be made with the kitten's mouth firmly clamped around a nipple. The reassurance purring by mother and littermates reduces movement and keeps the young in the nest.

The sharp, protractable claws of the kittens may be one reason for the purring. In settling the young down quickly, the mother is less likely to have her teats lacerated by scrambling kittens. Viverrids share with cats the otherwise unique protractable claws.

Males provide a huge territorial area within which females range. However, males do not provide food, so the female rears her young alone and hunts on a solitary basis. Purring among the young kittens while she is away from the nest will keep them together. When she returns to feed them, the mutual purring sustains their quiet closeness.

Much of the mother's time is taken up by nursing the kittens in a hostile world. It is vital that some *quiet* continuous signal can be used to inhibit kitten movement and noise.

The purr is also a statement from the kitten that says "I am here, I am here..." It is this statement of existence in the purr that is noticeable when a cat is snoozing unseen under a duvet and you sit on the bed. Suddenly up comes a purr, not as a sign of contentment or greeting but as a statement that "I am here." It is in its anxious form as an expression of existence that the vet often encounters purring upon examining a cat.

When cats purr on our laps, most of the behavior, as Darwin appreciated, is neotenous, as the cats are made to feel like kittens by our large, maternal-sized, warm lap. We do the equivalent of licking them by stroking them with our hands. We are reinforcing our bond with them, for a cat family that purrs together stays together.

Cat Etiquette

If you have difficulty "making friends" with strange cats, you can be placed in the awkward situation of visiting friends who say, "Oh you like cats, don't you? You'll love Binny," and Binny disappears.

We can be so keen yet simultaneously anxious that the cat is alarmed. Remember that communication is two-way. Ensure that you are not threatening and acknowledge cat politeness.

Don't charge in at your full height — squat down. Initially, extend your arm low down, with your index finger only stretched toward, but not reaching, the cat. Once the cat has accepted that, advance your finger so that the cat brings its nose forward to investigate. It will then usually recognize your finger as the "nose" of your hand, which is cat-head size, and simultaneously as a finger that it will use like a scent stick, rubbing its mouth against its point. Only then tickle its head, and even a shy cat will usually accept you, and your friends' response will be one of surprise: "Oh Binny doesn't usually like strangers; she can tell you're a real cat person." Your credibility will have shot up.

In a room of strangers cats often go to the person who is scared of cats and sit on his or her lap. This perversity

results from their perception that the stock-still person will be less inclined to hassle them. Consequently, do not overdo the stroking of cats on your first meeting because they are sizing you up.

There are also ways of relaxing cats at

Many owners recognize the stress relief they gain from cat companionship in a troubled world.

reassurance. Your cat will respond in like manner — direct communication. Similarly, a long yawn is a useful addition. With all cat communication, there is the appropriateness of doing the right thing at the right time.

Facial Expressions and Body Posture

The cat's range of expressions is not limited to vocalization. A whole range of facial and body positions has specific meanings, and the cat's ability to mix them allows it a wide spectrum, which is superimposed upon the vocal component. Paul Leyhausen established a gradation of both body postures and facial expressions that show a recognizable span, from fully defensive positions through a neutral position to full threat-of-attack positions.

In extreme defensive mode, the cat's ears are flattened to its head so that they almost disappear. In contrast, when a cat is aggressively moving toward a confrontation, its threat to attack can be read from the oblique angle of its body in the move, its head held down slightly, and its ears drawn around so that the backs can be seen from the front. The aggressor initiating a fray will often be poised to lift up its front paws onto its opponent. As it moves forward, its rear will be angled higher than its front. The cat anticipating such an attack, as well as flattening its ears, will also usually lower its head and shoulders, which will allow it to take a floor dive where it can defend itself by raking its hind legs back against the expected launched attack. The relative balance between aggressor and

a distance that I have established from working with feral cats for years, and they work just as well with house cats. A long, hooded, leisurely blink is very calming and used reciprocally between cats when they are settling as mutual defender can fluctuate during both the build-up and the combat if it occurs.

Mock battles can break out in quite vigorous "games" between adult cats. They can become ritualized, in that unexpectedly the cat initiating the sequence may be the "defender," which induces the "attacker" to take part, and the "battle" can become an excuse for a race around the house.

Stroke That Stress Away

Cats are good for you. Stroke a cat, and your stress levels drop. The people who need cats most are doctors, for they have around the highest suicide, divorce, and stress levels of any profession. Physician heal thyself — get a cat.

For some years research has shown that pet ownership is good for your health, and the study of "companion animals" has become respectable.

The Cats Protection League surveyed owners and found that the reduction of stress and the relief from depression and anxiety were major perceived advantages of living with a cat. Many long-term psychiatric hospitals and old people's homes have had resident or stray cats whose company has been enjoyed. Dennis is the "official cat" at the Luciel Van Geest Center in Peterborough, England, where Staff Nurse Pamela Baines finds that certain patients put significant effort into his care. She also finds that he "certainly helps to relax and calm stressed or agitated" patients. The Cats Protection League discovered that "eight out of ten caring organizations found that cats helped people get better."

Pets help institutionalized or isolated

people feel more comfortable and are a reminder of normal home life. The cat's silky coat makes it more strokable than the rougher texture of a dog's coat, which is more likely to be patted.

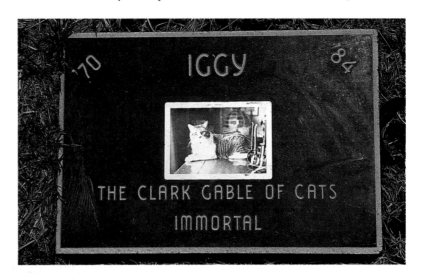

At the End of the Day

While the sentiments on burial plaques to cats can sometimes bring a smile to the face, few people are so hard-hearted that they cannot recognize the real feelings that reside there.

Putting a memorial over a cat's grave is not a new idea, for one of the most celebrated tombs was erected by Madame de Lesdiguières in the 17th century. On the mausoleum the cat's likeness was carved in marble and placed on a marble pillow. This was at a time when the cat was beginning to be accepted at the French court. It tangibly marked that point in the history of the cat when in Europe it began to enter a new relationship with us and to change from being considered a necessary evil to being valued as a loved companion.

A gravestone to a cat in Los Angeles shows how an owner reacted to the loss of his cat. Our relationship with our cat does not stop when contact turns to memory. In some cities in the United States, it is illegal for pets to be buried in your own garden, and pet cemeteries are common. For housebound cats it can be the first and last time they leave their owners' homes.

Further Reading

Alderton, David. *Wild Cats of the World* (Blandford, 1993)

Armitage, P., and Clutton-Brook, Juliet. "A Radiological and Historical Investigation into the Mummification of Cats from Ancient Egypt," *J. Arch. Sc.* 8: 185–96 (1981)

Baldwin, James. "Ships and the Early Diffusion of the Domestic Cat," *Carnivore Genetics Newsletter* 4: 32–33 (1979)

Borchelt, Peter, and Voith, Victoria. "Aggressive Behaviour in Dogs and Cats," *Compendium on Continuing Ed.* 7: 11 (1985)

Churcher, Peter, and Lawton, J. "Predation by Domestic Cats in an English Village," *J. Zool. Lond.* 212: 439–55 (1987)

Conway, William. *Dawn of Art in the Ancient World* (Percival, 1891)

Elton, C. "Cats in Farm Rat Control," *Brit. J. Animal Behav.* 1: 151–55, (1953)

Ewer, R. F. *The Carnivores* (Weidenfeld and Nicolson, 1973)

Gebhardt, Richard. *A Standard Guide to Cat Breeds* (Macmillan, 1979)

Karsh, Eileen. "The Effects of Early and Late Handling on the Attachment of Cats and People," in *"The Pet Connection" Conference Proceedings*, ed. Anderson, R., Hart, B., and Hart, L. (Globe Press, 1983)

Leyhausen, Paul. *Cat Behaviour* (Garland STMP Press, 1979)

Loxton, Howard. *The Noble Cat* (Merehurst, 1990)

Macfarlane, A. "Witchcraft Prosecutions in Essex 1560–1680," Ph. D. thesis (Oxford Univ., 1967)

Mead, Chris. "Ringed Birds Killed by Cats," *Mammal Rev.* 12:4 183–86 (1987)

Naville, Edouard. "Bubastis 1887–1889," *8th Memoir of the Eygpt Exploration Fund* (Kegan Paul Trench, 1891)

Robinson, Roy. *Genetics for Cat Breeders* (Pergamon Press, 1977)

Seidensticker, John, and Lumpkin, Susan. *Great Cats* (Merehurst, 1991)

Simpson, Frances. *The Book of the Cat* (Cassell, 1903)

Stahl, Philippe. "Le Chat Forestier d'Europe (*F. silvestris*): Exploitation des Resources et Organisation Spatiale" (Centre National d'Etudes sur la Rage et la Pathologie des Animaux Savages, 1986)

Tabor, Roger. *Cats: The Rise of the Cat* (BBC Books, 1991)

Tabor, Roger. "The Changing Life of Feral Cats at Home and Abroad," *Zool. J. Linnean Soc.* 95: 151–61 (1989)

Tabor, Roger. "General Biology of Feral Cats" in *The Ecology and Control of Feral Cats* (Universities Federation for Animal Welfare, 1981)

Tabor, Roger. *The Wild Life of the Domestic Cat* (Arrow, 1983)

Todd, Neil. "Cats and Commerce," *Scientific Amer,* 237: 100–7 (1977)

Turner, Dennis, and Bateson, Patrick. *The Domestic Cat* (Cambridge Univ. Press, 1988)

Weir, Harrison. *Our Cats and All About Them* (Clements, 1889)

Acknowledgments

The writing of this book has developed from around 20 years of my working as a cat biologist and behaviorist. Both for my researches and for television, the cat has taken me to many countries around the world. This has enabled me to pull from a large well of information in writing the book, into which many people have kindly contributed. I cannot possibly thank here everyone who has been involved over the years, and I hope that anyone I cannot squeeze in will nonetheless accept my thanks.

Special thanks are due to Sue Hall, Susie Hallam, Sue Cleave, Piers Spence, and everyone at David & Charles in producing this book as a happy collaboration. Also, for the *Understanding Cats* series, thanks are due to Jenny Cropper at the BBC, and Colin Tennant, John Bowe and my colleagues at Cats on Film/Avalon Productions. Thanks are also due to Dick Meadows and the BBC *Cats* team; Joan Moore and Malcolm Colchester at Cat World; the British Museum (Natural History) plus Ornithology section at Tring; the British Museum (Egyptology Dept.); Cairo Museum; Dept. of Antiquities,

Egypt; National Museum of Thailand; Cat Survival Trust; Zagazig University; Van University; North East London Polytechnic (now East London University); Universities Federation for Animal Welfare; Dudwa National Park, India; Pettrac; Colchester Zoo; TICA (New York and Los Angeles); the Cats' Protection League HQ staff and the CPL shelters at Battlesbridge and White Notley, especially Olive Hammond and Julie Kircher; Alley Cat Allies in the U.S., particularly Louise Holton and Becky Robinson; Holly Hazard and the Doris Day Animal League; Wendy Horn and Manx National Heritage; Helena Sanders and all at Venice DINGO; Christine Pierson and Cats Assistance to Sterilize, Australia; Doris Westwood and the Fitzroy Square Frontagers and Garden Committee; Debbie Rijinders and Ineke Aldendorff of Stichting De Zwerfkat, Holland; Lord and Lady Fisher; Stuart Baldwin, Fossil Hall; Karen Heinick, Florida State University; Brian McNerney and friends; the London cast of *Cats* and the Really Useful Company; the veterinary surgeons Alan Hatch and Jenny Remfry; Alain Zivie; Roy Robinson;

Charles Llewelyn and family; Juliet Clutton-Brook; Major General Pengrpicha; Joan Hodge; Mike Jackson; Harry Bourne; Kutbettin Bahadir; Ann Baker; Peter Churcher; Rachel and the Cooke family; Hank and DD Tyler; Sarah King; Michael Harding; Robin Kiashek and Georgie Oldroyde; Ed and Malee Rose; Gay Frank; Bob, Vally, and Charlotte Hudson; Jackie and Barry Wood; Solveig Pfluger; Dawn Gulliver; Mrs. A. Wright; Wendy Thornton; Jean Murchison; Ros Elliot; Bernice Mead; Barbara Castle; Anne Bailey; Sharon McAllister; Mr. and Mrs. A. Gilbert.

Finally it gives me especial pleasure to record my particular thanks to Liz Artindale, without whose hard work and considerable support this book would have taken far longer to prepare, and whose photographic skills have much enhanced its appearance.

I have delighted in the acquaintance of many cats during my researches giving rise to this book — particularly my past cat Mr. Jeremy Fisher and my present pair, Tabitha and Leroy.

ROGER TABOR

Index (Page numbers in *italics* indicate illustrations)